Role of Satellite Sites for The Growth of Arikamedu As Indo-Roman Trading Station

Role of Satellite Sites for The Growth of Arikamedu As Indo-Roman Trading Station

Dr. Arunraj T.

AGAM KALA PRAKASHAN
DELHI

First Published 2015

ISBN : 978 -81-7320-141-7

Published by:
Dr. Agam Prasad, M.A., Ph.D., Diploma in Museology
For **Agam Kala Prakashan**
34, Central Market, Ashok Vihar
Delhi - 110 052
Tel.: 27212195, 65688806-7
Fax: 91-11-27212195
Email: agambooks@gmail.com, agambook@yahoo.com
www.agamkala.com

Composed by:
Aman Printographics
Delhi - 110 052
Mobile: 9891395309

Printed by:
Chawla Offset Printers
Wazirpur Village, Ashok Vihar
Delhi-110 052

Printed in India

Dedicated to people of
Ancient village, Arikamedu

Contents

Preface

Unlike North India the Southern part of India especially Tamil region during the early historical period is well determined by trade activities rather than religious or political aspects in order to demark any urbanization existed here. For a proper understanding of the evolution of urbanism during this early historical period, we must consider the interaction between the metropolitan centers and various hinterland settlements (resource bases and productive units).

While long distance trade held between metropolitan centers of South India and outside world can be attested through the literary as well as archaeological remains, we did not pay much time to understand the local/ Hinterland trade. Because any long-distance trade exchange can be achieved as the result of numerous small distance (i.e. domestic) transfers.

Turing to Arikamedu, the most famous archaeological site in the South, was not fashioned by the minds of Romans, but was always at heart of a megalithic area and transformed as Romans trading station only in later part. But how arikamedu relates to any of the known sites (inland centers) in its immediate vicinity during pre Roman as well as Roman period is still not clear. So the main purpose of this book is to place before the scholars about identification of the some of the regional Centres around arikamedu, which may help us to know how Arikamedu benefited by these hinterland centers. During last 02 decades many scholars surveyed, the hinterland of Arikamedu and identified enough habitational sites containing cultural elements of Iron Age and succeeded by early historical sites. These recent researches helped to identify nearly 50-60 Satellite Settlements around Arikamedu, which were acted as hinterland trade centers of Arikamedu. Besides the present author also identified about 14 satellites sites in and around Arikamedu. Following these latest researches on Arikamedu, debate has now started among these scholars over the inland transshipment of commodities that reached Arikamedu for export purpose, and the imported commodities of arikamedu that distributed to the inland urban centers. While paradoxly, it has been concluded that the imported goods were fully consumed by the arikamedu settlers and all the exported goods were produced from Arikamedu and surrounding area.

Generally the size of these sites ranges from 5-50 acres, and show some sort of hierarchy between them. And presence of more sites in Pambai valley also suggests that inland transshipment was not only carried along the river Gingee but it was also in the banks of Pambai beyond Suttukeni and Tiruvakkarai.

So the research carried by me in the coming pages will be usefull for the readers to of identify strategic location of Arikamedu in the context of Megalithic exchange system and their interaction with the other early historical sites including North India.

I am grateful to my teacher Prof. Ravi Korisettar, Dharwad University, Karnatak to allow me to do research on this important topic. This book has been compiled to suit young researchers who wish to carry out similar studies with other major roman sites of India.

Readers are welcome to point out of any errors of omission or commission or give valuable suggestions for update this book to enhance its usefulness.

Acknowledgement

This book would not have seen the light of day without the help and encouragement of Prof. Ravi Korisettar, My research guide. I express my sincere thanks and gratitude to him for his guidance, care and support at all times.

I am grateful to Sh. K.S. Ramchandran, Dr. C. Margabandhu, Dir (Rtd), Sh. B.M. Pande, Dir (Rtd), Dr. (Late) B. Narasimaiah, Prof. K. Rajan, Prof. (Rtd). A. Ekambaranathan, Prof. A. Sundara, Prof. Alok Tripathi, Dr. D. Dayalan, Dr. Nambirajan, Dr. S Suresh, Dr. Selvakumar, Dr. Rajavelu, Sh. K.T. Gandhirajan and Sh. Ravi Chandrane, who boosted my interest in the research subject .

I owe my thanks to Dr. Rakesh Tiwari, Director General , ASI and Sh/s. S.B. Ota, Regional Director, Bhopal, Chandra Pandiyan (Dy. Sup. Chemist), Anil (AA), Muvendan (AA, Hampi), Librarian K. Rajan, Modeler N. Baskar, Surveyores Vinayagam & Kuppuswamy, Draughtsman Raghavendar, Perumal, CA(Rtd.), Ranjith, Basker, Veera ragavan, Ramesh, steno A.K. Pal and my assistant Satayamurthy for their ready help.

Special thanks to Ramesh & Sridhar (both from Villupuram), Annaduarai (Cuddalore), Narayana Murthy (Bank Manager from Vadalur), teacher couple Mr. Veera Ragavan and Mrs. Mangaiarkarasi (from Villupuram) to accompany me during the course of field work in the study area and discussed various aspects of the present research.

To my friends - Janardhana, Shankar Poojar, Jinu, Kalyan and Udayashakar - I owe a lot for all those days of fun and stress that we shared together during the filed work.

Looking back, I remember my parents Shri A. Thangasamy and Smt. Maragatham with immense respect, without their constant support and encouragement I would not have reached this stage. To them I dedicate this work. My two brothers & one sister and my lovable wife showed equal interest in my work and also helped me in many ways. I owe them a debt of gratitude. Thanks are due to all those whom I met during my visit to gather information about Arikamedu and its Satellite settlements.

Dr. Arun Raj. T

Foreword

Identified with the port of Podouke mentioned in the Periplus of the Erythraen Sea, the ancient site of Arikamedu in Puduchchery has been subjected to excavations since the forties of the last century. The site is also mentioned by Ptolemy. With the discovery of ancient remains and distinctly Roman antiquities found in and around the place, Arikamedu's identification as a trading centre has been clearly established. These distinctly Roman antiquities are the Arretine and Rouletted wares, amphorae, a Graeco-Roman gem with the head of Augustus in intaglio, Roman lamp of fine red ware and red ware sherds bearing on the base letters VIBII (VIBIE or VIBIF) CAMVRI and ITTA and finally an oblong building identified as a warehouse clearly suggesting its identification as an Indo-Roman trading station. Coupled with these distinctly Roman antiquities, the site also yielded other remains like a well, a ring-well, cisterns or vats, typical grey ware, black-and-red ware some of which bear inscriptions in graffito in early Tamil, all suggesting a flourishing settlement which served as an Indo-Roman trading station between the first century BCE and second century CE.

Arikamedu had been subjected to excavations by the French and American archaeologists; the Archaeological Survey of India excavated the site in 1945 and provided firm chronology of the settlement. While these earlier works were site specific, the present work Role of Satellite sites for the growth of Arikamedu as Indo- Roman trading station *by Dr. Arun Raj T. is based on field work and detailed study of the site in relation to various hinterland settlements which served as the resource base for this flourishing site.*

As a background to his field work, Dr. Raj has discussed the theoretical issues including analysis of centre-periphery relationships, the environmental factor including the topography, drainage system, geology, and flora and fauna of the area. With this theoretical background and analysis of the available material and keeping in view the salient features of urbanization during early historical period in Tamil Nadu, he has been able to present a cogent picture of the site. He has also tried to explain how and why Arikamedu emerged as an important centre of trade and commerce on the Coromondal coast and how it was related to inland settlements in the interior which served as resource base and production units. Based on his extensive field work and by analyzing site distribution, Dr. Raj has reconstructed early historic settlement pattern of Arikamedu and its satellite settlements which, according to him, were the backbone of the entire trade web. He has also shown how these small settlements specialized in craft activities such as extraction of semi-precious stones and other materials and harnessing the local forest resources.

Dr. Arun Raj carried out extensive explorations covering an area of 100 kms along the banks of the Gingee, Middle Pennaiyar, Vellar and Manimukha rivers and their major tributaries. In the course of this field work, he discovered 14 early historic sites and reexamined 29 sites. He has also been able to bring out the trade and cultural links between the megalithic and early historic settlements. In his view, Arikamedu's position as a centre of trade goes back even earlier than the commencement of Indo-Roman trade and that south-eastern India had a large trading network of coastal and inland ports and market centres that were intimately linked with Arikamedu.

Dr. Arun Raj's work is of great value to all those who are engaged in the study of trade networks. This work, in particular, assumes significance for his detailed analysis and exposition thereby unraveling the relationship of the centre and the peripheral sites. I commend this work to all those interested in this subject.

B. M. Pande
Director (Rtd.)
Archaeological Survey of India

List of Figures

List of Plates

CHAPTER 1

INTRODUCTION

Archaeological investigation into the Early Historic (BC 300-500 AD) settlement patterns, social and religion institutions, agrarian system, craft tradition and urbanism is crucial to tracing the evolution of modern Tamil culture as a distinctive cultural entity (Fig.01). For a proper understanding of the evolution of urbanism during the Early Historical period, we must consider the interaction between the metropolitan centers and various hinterland settlements (resource bases and production units), which maintained feedback relations. The long coastline of Tamil Nadu facilitated maritime trade, which could be traced back to later prehistoric (Megalithic) and Early Historic times. Cultural developments typical of the Early Tamilakam appear to have been governed by maritime contacts beyond its frontiers with a well-defined intra-regional trade network.

Arikamedu and a group of satellite settlements, in a radius of 100 sq. km. constitute the area of study primarily for its location amidst a number of megalithic as well as early historical sites. The archaeological evidence reveals that Arikamedu had trade links with a number of Megalithic and other Early Historic settlements of the region. Arikamedu and other Megalithic settlements were located on river banks for enabling transportation through boats to be able to establish a web of trade communication in the region. At several sites of megalithic way of life survived even after the onset of external trade, especially with Rome links with Rome. This is attested by the evidence of Roman coins, various household goods buried in Megalithic graves as far inland as Coimbatore. Thus, Arikamedu's position as a premier trade center appears to date from prior to the Indo-Roman period. The Romans selected this place as their trading port on account of its proximity to the sea and its links with hinterland.

Therefore, the present study aims at understanding the relationship between Arikamedu and its satellite settlements in a geographical perspective. They functioned together contributing to the economic development of the Iron Age society and its transformation through time.

1.1. Background

The site of Arikamedu is situated on the Coromandel Coast of southeast India, 4 Kms south of Pondicherry, within the Union Territory of Pondicherry (Fig.02). A French astronomer, Guillaume Le Gentil who had visited Pondicherry in 1768-71, records that along the high bank of the Ariyankuppam River, diggings had revealed some 10 ft. high walls, built with large-size bricks, which were one foot long and seven to eight "thumbs" large, and were put together with mud mortar (le Gentil 1779, 2: 109-111). He also mentions seeing vestiges of wells exposed along the high river bank, which, according to him, were originally at least 20 feet deep and 4 feet wide, made from a serious of earthenware vessels placed above each other (Ibid.). The reference is, no doubt, to terracotta ring wells, a large number of which have been found in later excavations too. Le Gentil (Ibid.) considered the ruins to be the remains of an ancient town or large village which, according to the local residents known as Virampattinam. Accordingly, on his map of Pondicherry, he identifies it as such.

Jouneau-Dubreuil's (1941:449) identification of the Arikamedu site with Poduke emporium mentioned in the Periplus Mari Erythraei (PME) is accepted by historians; thus, the name Poduke, perhaps deriving from Tamil Puducheri, meaning new hamlet (the origin of the name Pondicherry), must have been in use at the time of the Periplus, believed to be ca. the middle to the second half of the first century AD (Casson 1989:6-7). Since the meaning of the Tamil word puducheri implies a new settlement or, at least a change, it has been suggested that the name Puducheri was perhaps given when the settlement was transformed from a small village (name unknown) into a center of commerce (Wheeler 1954: 146-7). If so, this must have occurred before the Periplus was written. Arikamedu, the name used by Wheeler, and by which name the site is best known today, is the local name for the mound.

The historical importance of the site and its connection with the Roman Empire was first recognized by Jouveau-Dubreuil, who had started collecting artifacts from the surface of the mound and the river bank as early as 1937. Several French scholars associated with the Ecole Francaise de Extreme-Orient and the Hanoi Museum also visited the site. In the year 1939, M. Goloubew is said to have found a carnelian gem, possibly from a signet ring. It reportedly depicted the head of Augustus in intaglio (Pattabiraman 1946: 15-16; Fikkiozat 1949: 18). Later in 1940 Krishnaswami Gownder, owner of aplot of land along the northern river front, dug an area of 60 X 30 m to a depth of 0.80 m for the puspose o planting coconut trees (Pattabiraman 1946: 15-16). From the debris, several artifacts were collected, including fragments of shipping amphora's, which were brought to the attention of Jouveau-Dubrevil. In the same year, A. Aiyappan, Government Museum, Chennai, was published by him in an article "A Dakshina Taxila, Historic Relics from Arikamedu", The Hindu (March 23, 1941). Several other Indian scholars visited the site at about the same time.

Between1941-44, however, small-scale excavations were undertaken by French scholars under the direction of L. Faucheux and R. Sarleau; the latter also plotted two grids, oriented north-south, for what were considered to be the most significant areas for excavations. Parts of the site were also declared protected by the French Government (Pattabiraman 1946: 19). These excavations were partially published in a brief report by Faucheaux in 1945 and by Pattabiraman in 1946. They were also summarized in the annual administrative reports of the Pondicherry Government, mentioned above. However, the most outstanding excavations were conducted by the Archaeological Survey of India under the direction of Mortimer Wheeler during a short season in the summer of 1945 with the extensive resources of the ASI at his disposal, since he was its Director General (Wheeler et al., 1946; Wheeler, 1951, 1954, 1976).

Wheeler's excavations at Arikamedu were the most widely known, both in India and outside, partly because of the methodology followed by him, and partly because of the publicity given to the excavations by Wheeler himself in his numerous publications. Among them the most frequently cited one is Rome beyond the Imperial Frontiers (1954). An important contribution of Wheeler's work at Arikamedu was the preparation of a contour map of the site and the surrounding area, which was included in the excavation report (Wheeler et al., 1946: pl. VIII).

J.M. Casal continued excavation here in 1947 a fairly extensive area, more than any other archaeologist. During his three excavation seasons extremely valuable data were obtained, but published only selectively (Casal 1949; Casal and Casal 1956). Casal's excavations, unfortunately, went largely unnoticed. Wheeler very briefly mentions Casal's findings in his publications after 1951 (Wheeler, 1954: 146-47). Whereas archaeologists in India have usually not cited Casal's work.

After a comprehensive review of archaeological work at Arikamedu Vimala Begley initiated fresh excavation in the early 1990s (1989-92). It was a joint Indian-American effort. The renewed excavations revealed many new types of artifacts and structures. These have proved, beyond doubt that the site was first occupied during the second century BC and the height of the region's trade with the Mediterranean was from 50 BC to AD 50 (see Begley, 1996, 2004).

Recent Under Water Investigation at Arikamedu

In the middle of 2002 a team of archaeologists from the ASI, including those from the marine archaeology wing and Chennai Circle carried out under water survey (Tripathi, 2002a: 74-107; Tripathi, 2002b: 146-149). This survey revealed that impact of erosion on the site and the original extent of the site was beyond the present limits.

Excavations at Arikamedu (conducted between 1945 and 1992) have brought to light the existence of small and large industries during the Pre-Roman period. Large quantities of worked and unworked shell, beads and pottery clearly indicated the existence of indigenous craft traditions prior to the arrival of Romans. Megalithic sites in the Gingee, Vaigai-Tamraparni and Kaveri Valleys support the economic activity at Arikamedu. Shell cutting and pearl fishing were a major area of occupation of the people at many of the sites.

Chronology

Wheeler dated the site with the help of imported pottery viz. Arretine Ware and amphora from the Mediterranean. He found that almost all the excavated structures were constructed in the post of the Arretine ware period indicating that the site came to occupied during the first two centuries AD (Wheeler et al., 1946: 24). The presence of Celadon Ware and Chola coins of eleventh century AD indicated a long occupation of the site (Wheeler et al., 1946: 91). Excavations in 1989-1992 brought to light evidence of trade with the Mediterranean in third to seventh century AD, as well as occupation during the Chola period and contact with Southeast Asia through trade (Begley, 1996: 30-35).

The evidence of Celadon ware clearly supports the idea that ships from India were engaged in trade with China. Probably the site lost its importance in the first half of the fourteenth century when a sand bar was formed at the mouth of Ariyankuppam River, which blocked the entry of ships to the river, and this important port fell in disuse.

Structures

Wheeler divided the entire site in two parts, northern sector and southern sector. The nature and date of the structures unearthed in these two sectors also varied. The structures at Arikamedu were made of bricks, which not survive the natural hazards.

The northern sector contained the remains of a substantial structure built about 50 AD. This building was identified as a warehouse. The warehouse was built on the foreshore of the estuary on which apparently timber buildings had already stood. The debris of port penetrated into it (Wheeler et al., 1946: 24-26). The brickwork with mud mortar had tough plaster outside to keep out water on this low-lying site. It must have been liable to flooding and was abandoned at an early date.

After AD 50, there were several suggestive stages of construction and reconstruction. The southern sector was occupied for about a hundred years or more. Occupation at the site continued till 200 AD. Main structures constructed in the southern sector were two walled courtyards, with carefully built dyeing vat tanks supplied and drained by a series of brick culverts. Extensive use of drain, substantial pavements of large bricks and the absence of domestic features suggest its use for industrial purposes. Excavator conjectured that these tanks and courtyards were used in the preparation of the muslin cloth.

Besides, excavations conducted by French scholars and Wheeler unearthed several other structures. These were small in size, unconnected and fragmentary in nature. Some of these fragmentary structures found in excavations were drains constructed by means of corbelled walls, floored and roofed with horizontal bricks, a number of fragmentary walls, patches of brick floor, a fragmentary square or oblong structure of uncertain purpose, blocks of brickworks and pavements, ring-well or soak-pit built of pottery rings (Wheeler et al., 1946: 24), etc. Since these structures were very small in size and not connected with other structures it was not possible to ascertain their use or purpose.

Stratigraphy

Stratigraphy in the southern and northern sectors varies. Due to vandal digging and extensive damage caused to it the stratigraphic sequence is not clear. In the southern sector natural soil was found at 3 m. above the sea level. It was out of reach of flood. Habitation started here later but continued after abandonment of northern sector (Wheeler et al., 1946: 27). The cultural deposits were divided in three main phases - Early Middle and Late which were further divided in sub-periods. There was continuity of occupations throughout.

The Problem

Despite several excavations during the last century many questions regarding origin, development and extension of this town, chronology, ancient port, trade mechanism, etc., are as yet not satisfactorily answered. How and why Arikamedu became an important centre of commerce on the Coromondal Coast needs to be explained. The excavations were conducted in limited area with limited aims. Except two structural complexes, the other structures unearthed were fragmentary in nature. Some of the areas excavated by Wheeler and Casal have suffixed a great deal of damage.

Further, how Arikamedu was related to inland interior settlements and what type of political or economic organization may have governed the location of the port needs to be explained.

Whereabouts of Arikamedu Artifacts

Artifacts unearthed from Arikamedu, from time to time are now in various museums and private collections across the world. Perhaps, no other site can claim the distinction of having its artifacts distributed among a large number of individuals and institutions.

A part of Jouveau-Dubreuil's collection is in the Government Museum at Egmore, Chennai. A few of the early finds by the French were sent to the French Museum at Hanoi and Louvre Museum in Paris. Some objects from the early French excavations (1941-43) are reported to have been given to State Government museums in Bangalore and Hyderabad in South India. Yet, at least some of the material from these digs appears to have been lost. Most of the material from Wheeler's excavation is in the collection of the ASI at Purana Qila in New Delhi while others are in the collection of Institute of Archaeology, London. More materials from the site are in the collections of the Government Museum, Chennai and the British Museum, London. The selected materials unearthed during the excavations conducted by V. Begley's team in 1989-1992 are with the ASI, Chennai. A small collection of Arikamedu objects is in the Aurobindo Ashram Library at Pondicherry.

Arikamedu through the Ages

One can reconstruct the long and interesting history of Arikamedu by piecing together information from multiple sources such as archaeology, Sangam and Western literature.

The occasional finds of stone axe with pointed butts, both on the surface and in the archaeological trenches, at Arikamedu, suggested a Neolithic substratum at the site (around 4000 BC?). The use of such stone hand-axes during later periods was also known in many other South Indian sites (Suresh 2008: 57).

As per the latest archaeological evidence, the site was first occupied, on a regular basis, around the late third century or early second century BC. This period belongs to the Late Iron Age or Megalithic Age in South

India. The earliest habitation was in the Southern sector and not in the Northern Sector. Fishing and bead-making were important occupations of this community.

We are not sure about as to when exactly Arikamedu began its trade with the Mediterranean region. Probably, the trade started, on the modest scale, around the second century BC., soon after the occupation of the site. But trade was at its height from the mid-first century BC to mid-first century AD. During this period, the site may have been a part of Sangam Chola Kingdom that had its capital further south at Uraiyur. Significantly, a square copper coin of this dynasty has been found during V. Begley's archaeological digs (1989-92) at Arikamedu. Alternatively, Arikamedu would have been a part of the territory of the Malaiyaman chieftain who controlled the regions close to Arikamedu with Tirukoilur as their capital. Or else, the Velir chieftains ruled the region. Perhaps, each of these dynasties controlled Arikamedu, one after the other. At this point of time, both the Northern and Southern Sectors were occupied, probably by different ethnic communities (Suresh, 2008). There was continuous interaction between the occupants of the two sectors. The site evolved into an urban industrial centre where different types of pottery, beads, ivory artifacts and textiles were produced. The industrial area was spread over both the sectors. The southern sector was also the main market place. The port, however, was located in the northernmost part of the Northern Sector. The settlement of Roman and other foreign traders and merchants was located in this sector. No wonder, the quantity of Mediterranean artifacts is much larger in this Sector than in the Southern Sector.

Towards the end of the first century AD the volume of trade decreased probably due to changes in the pattern of trade and trade routes. But the settlement did continue and new buildings were constructed between the third and sixth centuries AD. Bead-making continued to be an important industry. For trade activities of this period, there are evidences in the form of a few fragments of rare fifth century AD imported amphorae at the site. By now, the power of the Sangam Cholas and Malaiyamans declined and the site would have been under the control of the Pallava dynasty that ruled this region with Kanchipuram as its capital (Suresh, 2008: 58).

We have more concrete evidence for the occupation of the site between the tenth-eleventh and fourteenth-fifteenth centuries AD. These elements include beads, buildings and roof tiles. During this period, Arikamedu was a part of the vast empire of the Imperial Cholas. From the Cholas, the territory may have passed on to the Vijayanagar Empire that emerged as a major power in South India from 1336 to 1565 AD. Chola coins including those issued by Raja Raja I, have been frequently found at Arikamedu. Typical Chola pottery and mud lamps also occur at the site. A Chola period Buddhist sculpture has been reported from the neighborhood. During this period, the site appears to have again emerged as an international trade centre. The Chinese ceramics and coins unearthed at the site indicate that the site had brisk trade with China. There is a reference to the Arikamedu port in a Medieval Chinese text. Arikamedu's contacts with the Persia region are indicated by the occurrence of Persian blue glazed pottery (Suresh, 2008: 59).

Probably, the site was abandoned sometime in the sixteenth-seventeenth centuries. There are references to brick-robbing at the site in 1734.

Towards the end of the 18th century, after the French conquest of the area, the site was briefly reoccupied. In 1771-73, a seminary and residence was built for the Jesuit missionaries. Close physical examination of the seminary ruins has revealed that this building was mostly built with new bricks but interestingly, some old large bricks removed from structures of the Roman trade period (first century AD) were also used. The seminary was abandoned in 1783. The locals refer to the ruined seminary as the 'Mission House'. During this period, a few other buildings were also constructed at Arikamedu. Portions of these buildings were noticed during Casal's excavations at the site. This period saw the import of blue-and-white ceramics from China.

During the nineteenth and early twentieth centuries, the history of Arikamedu appears more obscure. Sometime during this period, large portions of the site came to be used for agricultural operations. Mango, Coconut and Tapioca were cultivated. Cultivation was allowed to continue even after the archaeological importance of the site was recognized and parts of the site declared a protected area.

In 1954, the French rule in Pondicherry ended. Now, the entire Pondicherry region including Arikamedu joined the Republic of India. Since then, Arikamedu has been a protected site of the ASI.

1.2. Aims and Scope of the Work

This research aimed to conduct investigations into (a) settlement pattern of Arikamedu and its satellite settlements; (b) evolution of urbanism in the region, particularly during the Indo-Roman period; (c) delineate the role of agriculture and crafts specialization and diversification at the sites; (d) a locational analysis of early rock-cut Jaina caves, bearing Tamil-Brahmi inscription and; (e) the importance of port settlements of Kaveripattinam and Korkai.

1.3. Methodology

The following research techniques have been adopted in this study :-

1.3.1 Archaeological Fieldwork

A thorough archaeological survey spanning five filed seasons from 2003-2008 was carried out in the river valleys of Gingee, Pannar and Vellar and its tributaries and distributaries. Village to village survey was conducted to discover Early Historic sites. Previously reported sites were re-visited during the survey. Topographic maps of 1.50000 scale, were studied before undertaking the survey.

1.3.2 Section Scraping

Section scraping was carried out at the site of Sengamedu or Nallur (near Virudhachalam) to assess the thickness of the habitation deposit on the Manimuktar river. Bridge construction across the river has caused disturbance of the site exposing antiquities of the Early Historic period.

1.3.3 Collection of Artifacts

A random collection of antiquities was made from the surface of the sites. Significant potsherds diagnostic to the period under study were selected after a detailed description of the contexts.

1.4 Analysis and Interpretation of Data

The following methods were used in data analysis, interpretation and reconstruction of the material culture of the sites in the study area:-

1.4.1 Theoretical and Methodological Studies

The data collected from the sites has been interpreted taken into account of modern models and methods. The zonal approach of Trigger (1968) has been adopted in the reconstruction of Early Historic settlement pattern. The ethnographic and the 'Centre and Periphery' models have been adopted while interpreting the Early Historic trade mechanism.

1.4.2 Review of Work on Arikamedu

Published literature on excavations has been used as secondary data source. Some of these publications are part of larger studies on ancient trade and economy. Except for the excavation reports, studies on the Arikamedu material have been few and far between until recent times. In 1952, a brief article on the dating of the Arretine Ware (terra Sigillata) was published by L. Ohlenroth (1952); studies of the Brahmi and Tamil-Brahmi inscriptions on potsherds by M.J. Filliozat (1947: 107-18; 1949: 1-29); a brief article on glass rods by B.B. Lal (1958); and archaeomagnetic studies of five bricks from the site by Ramaswamy et al. (1976-80). In the 1980s, there appears to have been a renewed scholarly interest in Arikamedu and a series of independent studies appeared. These include a study of the beads by Peter Francis, Jr. (1976-80, 1987, also 1991); I. Mahadevan's (1970, 1973, 1986) research papers on the ancient name and pottery inscriptions of Arikamedu; a study of the bead technology by John Gwinnett and Leonard Gorelick (1988); E. Marianne Stern's (1986, 1987, 1988) work on Roman Glass, and V. Begley's own work on the chronology of the ancient settlement and some of its pottery (Begley 1983, 1986, 1988) and Rome and India: The Ancient Sea Trade (Begley and De Puma, 1991) and S. Suresh's (2004) study of the pottery from Arikamedu in the wider context of the Roman and Pseudo Roman objects found in India. Besides, information has been availed from many scholars in the form of personal communications. In addition, ancient and colonial accounts have been thoroughly surveyed for collecting information on the study region.

CHAPTER TWO

ENVIRONMENTAL BACKGROUND

2.1. The Study Area

The area of study includes Arikamedu and its satellite settlements scattered across the Union Territory of Pondicherry, and Cuddlore and Villupuram districts (i.e. old South Arcot district) of Tamil Nadu (Fig.03 and 04). These regions have been surveyed, particularly along the rivers such as Gingee, Middle Pennar, Vellar and Manimuka and their major distributaries and tributaries. The total area of study is about 100 Sq. Kms.

2.1.1 Topography

Pondicherry Region

The region (Long. 79° 50' N and Lat. 11° 55' E) is a flat country with an average elevation of about 15 m AMSL intersected by the deltaic channels of the Gingee and Pennar and other streams forming the two main drainage basins. Lagoons, lakes and tanks are other topographic features.

The region under study constitutes four geographical areas: The coastal Zone comprising newer and older dunes including saline areas of clayey texture. The second zone is made up of the two plateau called

Pondicherry plateau and Tiruvakkari plateau made up of a geological formation called the 'Cuddalore sandstones'. The upper layers are made up of red ferralitic soil. The Valudavur plain lies between these two plateaus. Marshy depressions are also frequently encountered in the plains of Valudavur. The flat alluvial zone occupies the rest of the Pondicherry region.

South Arcot Region

The South Arcot region under study is situated between Long. 78° 3' 47" to 80" N and Lat. 11° 1' 48" to 12° 2' 42" E and occupies an area of 9700 Kms. It is bounded on the south and southeast respectively by Thanjavur and Trichy districts. The southern boundary follows for the great part of its length the course of two rivers– the Vellur and Kollidam. It is flanked on the north and northwest by Dharmapuri and Salem districts, on the north by Kanchipuram district and on the east by the Bay of Bengal. It comprises 13 taluks seven in Villupuram District and six in Cuddalore District. The Villupuram District occupying the western part of the region includes the taluks of Tindivanam, Tirukkoyilur, Gingee Kallakurichi, Tittakudi, Villupuram and Ulundurpettai. The Cuddalore, Chidambaram, Kattumannar koil, Panruti, Vanur and Virdhachchalam taluks are in Cuddalore District.

Most part of the district is a flat plain sloping gently towards the sea. The Kalrayans hills on the south-western border are a prominent geographic feature. The group of rocky heights which lies on the south-west of Gingee is called as Gingee hills.

Kalrayan Hills

These hills which divide Vallupuram district from Salem district stand on the extreme west of Kallakurichi taluk. Though the range looks level from below, it contains no true plateaus. Its valleys are eroded into basin-shaped depressions. The rivers Manimuktandi, the Gomukhandi and Mayuranadi constitute the drainage network.

Gingee Hills

The Gingee hills differ widely in appearance from Kalrayans. The range is made up of detached hills which run from near Gingee southwards for some 14 miles. There are few other hills namely perumukkal and Tiyaga Durg and also mt. Capper plateau.

2.1.2 Geology

The major part of the Tamil Nadu consists of an assemblage of crystalline rocks of gneissic series, which form the basement complex upon which later geological formative occur. The gneissic rocks have veins of quartz and limestone, which are both nodular and crystalline (Fig.05).

The Pondicherry region is occupied by Archeaeans (Charnokite), restricted to a small area and other formation ranging in age from the Cretaceous to Recent times. In this region the rocks may be divided into three categories (i) sandstone (ii) pebble and (iii) shale. In the alluvial tract of Pondicherry, clays suitable for manufacture of bricks, occur within 10 to 15 Kms, west-south-west of Pondicherry town. In the Red Hills (Gorimedu) area and the high-ground to the west of kalapet impersistent bands of shale are noticed. They are seen to contain clay varying from 75 to 90%. The clays are medium grained, soft and plastic.

The geological formations met with in South Arcot region are classified into give groups:-

1. Gneissic series
2. Cretaceous rocks
3. Cuddalore sandstones
4. Alluvial deposits
5. Tiruvakkarai fossils

The Gneissic rocks occupy the western part of the district. Eastwards of these are numerous clusters of detached hills, some of considerable size and elevation and remarkable for their bold forms and great ruggedness.

Fossiliferous Cretaceous lime stones are found exposed northwest of Vridhachchalam and west of Pondicherry. The fossils were first brought to the notice by K.C.Kaye in 1840.

Cuddalore Sandstone is characterized by its ferruginous nature. It occurs nearly Pelandurai, Virudhachalam, Parur, southeast of Tirukkoyilur and west of Cuddlore. The Cuddalore standstone formation is known as Mount Capper.

The sand formation to the west of Tiruvakkarai village exposed with a number of large masses of silicified wood. In 1810, Captain John Warren recorded 60 feet long tree trunk. Captain Newbold mentions the occurrence of 100 fet long trunk. This siliceous matter of petrification is often semi-transparent like chart. The inner portion of the tree has been usually more perfectly fossilized than the exterior.

The alluvial deposits are the most recent sedimentary formations, in the deltaic region of the rivers draining the region which are presently upraised some 20 feet above the sea level. But none of the rivers of this district are now farming deltas as the silt carried down by them is swept away by the strong current.

2.1.3 Soil

Pondicherry Region

Soil, coastal sands, alluvium and late rite cover a large part of the area.

Alluvium

The alluvial cover of the region betrays varying thickness. The alluvium of black compact clays. It simulates marine clay deposited to coastal swamps. The clayey material forms layers alternating with sand and has been met with in borings. Marine shells and oysters are also found in the clays. The alluvial deposits range in thickness between 15m and 68m. In the vicinity of Ariyankuppam-Thengathittu area it is reported to extend up to a depth of 40m. In the alluvial area the most commonly observed soil is a light brownish sandy loam.

In the area to the east of the Cuddalore-Pondicherry road, sandy soils are observed. Around Tirubhuvanai and Pallittennal also sands and sandy soils are developed.

Light brownish medium grained sand is observed along the coast between Pudukkupam and Pondicherry and east of Kalapet varying in which from 0.2 Km. to a maximum of 0.8 Km. The sands consist for the great part of quartz with small amounts of heavy minerals mostly magnetite and of epidotic. Two small patches with magnetite concentrated in fair amount are observed east-north-east of Nallavadu up to Virampattinam.

South Arcot Region

The soils of the district can be divided into three main classes, namely, the black or regur, the red ferruginous and arenaceous. They are distributed in the proportion of 35, 61 and 3 percent respectively in the total arable area. The remaining one percent represents the lands assessed at special rates during the resettlement and forms an exceptional serious. The black soil widespread in the Chidambaram, Vriddhachalam and Cuddalore taluks. The former two taluks along contain more than one half of the total extent of the soil in the district.

The red soil covers large extent of Gingee, Tirukkoyilur and Kallakkurichchi taluks, while the arenaceous soil occurs chiefly near the coast in the taluks of Chidambaram, Cuddalore and Tindivanam. Black clay is most fertile soil, followed by loam, red sand and arenaceous soils in that order. The black soil is impervious and retains moisture larger than others. Black brown soil is therefore the best soil for horticulture and rice cultivation. The red loam and sandy soils are more easily ploughed and require low rain fall for sowing and are best suited for dry hardy crops, chiefly groundnut and pulses. The arenaceous soil is suited for plantations, chiefly of casuarinas, cashew and coconut.

2.1.4 Drainage

The Gingee, Pennar, Gadilam, Vellar study area, almost all of them, flow to the east into the Bay of Bengal. The general description of the rivers described here.

2.1.4.1 Gingee

The Gingee River, also called Sankarabharani or the Varahanadi, rises in the Gingee taluk and flows past Gingee in a southerly course into the Villupuram taluk. Just as it enters the Villupuram taluk it receives on the left the Tondaiyar which also rises in the Gingee taluk and flows for a part of its course in the Tindivanam taluk. It then receives in the Villapuram taluk the Kallar and the Pambaiyar (or the Pombai) on the right, enters the erstwhile French province and finally into the Bay of Bengal with two distributaries near Pondicherry. The northern of these outlets is called the Ariyankuppam River, while the southern is known as Kilinjiyar or Chunambar. The Gingee River is fed by the monsoon. It is not nagivable and there are a series of anicuts across it.

The Prambaiyar rises in the Villupuram taluk, flows in an easterly direction and falls into the Gingee just as it is about to leave the taluk. Part of the courses of this jungle stream is utilized for the Pambai channel of the Ponnaiyar. A regulator put across it helps not a little to supply the tanks on either side for irrigation purposes.

2.1.4.2 Pennar

The pennar or the Ponnaiyar is the principal revier of the district. It rises in the Chenna Kesava hill, east of Nandidurg in Mysore, where it is known as the Southern Pinakini, in contradistinction to the Northern Pinakini which has its source close by. The name Ponnaiyar, by which the Southern Pinakini is usually known in the Tamil Nadu State, is said to be a corruption of the word Pennaiyar, the appellation by which it is described in ancient Tamil literature, but it is not known why the river was called Pennai which means a palmyra tree.

The Pennar flows southward for the most part of its course in Mysore and turning then slightly to the east makes its way through the Eastern Ghats and enters the Hosur taluk of Salem District. After traversing the district, it enters the southwest corner of the (old) North Arcot district, where it makes its way through the Chengam Pass between the Kalrayan Hills and Tenmalais and flows through Chengam and Tiruvannamalai taluks. It comes to the boundary of the South Arcot district near Mungilthuraipattu in the north of the Kallakkurichchi taluk, runs along the boundary of the Tiruvannamalai and Tirukkoyilur taluks with Kallakkurichchi taluk, flows past Parasapattu and receives on the right a small stream called Musukundanadi near Sripadanallur. It then enters the Tirukkoyilur taluk, flows past Trikkoyilur on its right and Arakanadanallur on its left, and receives on its left the Tirunjalar from the Tiruvannamalai taluk below Tirukkoyilur, about the anicut. In this part of its course, it shows an irresistible tendency to flow, especially when it is in high flood into the Malattar "barren river" which takes off from it on the right. It next flows along the boundary of the Villupuram taluk with the Triukkoyilur and Cuddalore taluks. Soon after it leaves the Tirukkoyilur taluk, another branch also known as the Malattar and sometimes called the Virukta Binasini, takes off from its left; and this branch flows through the Villupuram and the Cuddalore taluks and the former French enclaves in those taluks and falls into the sea at Madalapattu, some miles north of Cuddalore. The main river then flows for a short distance in the northern part of the Cuddalore taluk and finally falls into the sea, about 3 miles north of Cuddalore.

The Ponnaiyar runs in a wide sandy bed with low banks. Its supply depends more on the rainfall near its source in Mysore than on the rainfall in the district. It comes down in short floods which rapidly dry up and irrigation under it is mostly done by leading its freshens into storage tanks. There is an anicuts across it four miles below Tirukkoyilur.

The Malattar which, as has already been stated, takes off from the right of the Ponnaiyar in the Tirukkoyilur taluk, divides itself into two branches just as it is about the leave the taluk. Its southern and major branch flows through the eastern corner of the Cuddalore taluk and joins the Gadilam.

2.1.4.3 Gadilam

The Gadilam rises in the eastern part of the Tirukkoyilur taluk and receives a tributary on the right. It then enters the Cuddalore taluk where the Malattar comes and joins it on the right, flows past Panruti, and through Tiruvendipuram and Cuddalore and meets the Bay of Bengal, a mile north of Cuddalore. Just before it falls into the sea, it sends a small branch to the north which joins the sea north of Fort St. David.

The river carries fertile silt and there are four anicuts across the river which helps irrigation. In ancient days it was known as the Kedilam meaning a "deep gulf". It is also sometimes called the Garudanadi.

The Uppanar, or the Paravanar, has its source in the Vriddhachalam taluk, flows eastwards along the boundary between the Cuddalore and Chidambaram taluks and joins the Bay, to the south of Cuddalore Old Town. It is largely a drainage channel for the land irrigated by the Shatiatope anicut across the Vellar. Its water often backs up and floods the land along its sides. The Kudivaiyar is a small stream in the Cuddalore taluk which falls into the Uppanar close to its mouth near the Bay.

2.1.4.4 Vellar

The Vellar (white river) is formed by the junction of two rivers, namely, the Vasishtanadi and the Swetanadi (white river) which rise in the Salem District. The former which is named after sage Vasishta who is stated to have performed a sacrifice on its banks. The Swetanadi rises in the Kollimalai and drains the northern side of the Pachamalais in Salem. The Vasishtanadi enters the South Arcot district through the Attur Pass just south of the Kalrayans and forms for some sixteen miles boundary between that district and Trichy. After it joins Swetanadi, the boundary still follows for another 20 miles course of the united streams and then the Swetanadi, which now comes to be called the Vellar, strikes north-eastwards and flows through the Vriddhachalam taluk where it receives, about 4 miles east of Srimushnam, a considerable tributary, the Manimuktanadi, which is made up of the Mani and the Mukta streams that drain the northern part of the eastern slopes of the Mayuranadi and the Gomukhanadi (cow's mouth river) and the Mayuranadi (peacock river) that rise in the southern portion of the hills. These rivers have cut for themselves deep clefts with often precipitous sides in the valleys, notably in the Tumbe valley down which the Manimuktar flows. After it is joined by the Manimuktar, the Vellar flows through the Chidambaram taluk and joins into the sea immediately south of Porto Novo (Parangipettai). The Vellar receives little supply from the Southwest monsoon, but the North-East monsoon gives it adequate supply towards the later part of the year. Its banks are often high and steep, and are affected by the tide for about seven or eight miles above its mouth at Porto Novo (Parangipettai). It is navigable at this place and its waters are said to be impregnated with salts which are harmful, unless the supply is sufficient to prevent them from setting. It has anicuts at Shatiatope and Pelandurai and a regulator at Toludur.

There are some backwaters in the South Arcot region caused by the struggle between the sand-laden currents of the Bay and waters of the rivers trying to find an outlet into the sea. Another backwater is that of Marakkanam. This is filled with salt water when the small streams which drain the country behind it breach the sand spit, but when they are not strong enough to do so, it remains a brackish lagoon. It opens into the sea near ruined fort at Alamparai. Just south of this backwater is the swamp called the kaliveli (the empty plain), a dismal area, thirty one square miles in extent, which is dry for the greater part of the year and is covered with tussocks of coarse grass. Originally this seems to have formed part of the Marakkanam backwater. Near Porto

Nova (Parangipettai), again, there are other sand spits at a distance of four or five miles from the sea.

2.1.5 Climate

Pondicherry

Situated well within the tropics near 12° N Latitude on the east coast of India, Pondicherry experiences a hot and tropical maritime type of climate characterized by small variation in temperature, humid weather and moderate rainfall, but without a clear demarcation of seasons. The summer season lasts from March to October during which period the South West monsoons covers the region. However, the region receives relatively higher rainfall during the North East monsoon. The period from December to February is relatively cooler. During the north-east monsoon season, depressions and storms from the south Bay of Bengal move across or in the neighborhood causing heavy rain and thunder-storms and gusty winds. Tidal waves flooding the low lying coastal area accompany most of the storms. The average annual rainfall in Pondicherry is about of 127 cm. The relative humidity is generally high, being about 70 per cent during August to April. It is as its minimum value of 60 to 65 per cent in June and July.

The climate of the south Arcot region is characterized by an average rainfall. It is the heaviest along the coast and varies with the distance of each locality from the coast to inland. Porto Nove (Parangipettai) has usually the heaviest rainfall, followed by Chidambaram and Kallakurichchi. The north-east monsoon rainfall is more than double that of the south-west monsoon rainfall on the coast in Vriddhachalam taluk. The Gingee taluk and portions of Vriddhachalam, Kallakurichchi and Tirukkoyilur taluks. The latter constitute a rain shadow area. The average temperature for the period 1891-1940 recorded at Cuddalore is 82.7 and the hottest months are April to June and the coolest months are December and January. The highest recorded temperature during

1981-194 was 110° and the lowest 52°. The coastal parts of the districts are naturally moist and damp.

2.1.6 Vegetation

The earliest writing on the Indian flora commenced actually with Garcia da Orta. Between 1560 and 1610, he published his works on the Indian plants, in Portuguese and Latin Languages.

Pondicherry region

The flora of Pondicherry has a remarkable diversity which may be attributed to the intensity of rainfall and diverse soil types, comprising the hydromorph soils (rich in clay), the halomorphic soils (terrains more or less slatish), the sand-dunes and the very dry soils developed on the red sandstones of Kalapet, Dhanwantarinagar (Gorimedu) and Usteri. Added to this a large variety of exotic plants were introduced by the Europeans in the course of the last three centuries. This ecological diversity is also reflected in the land use.

The main dry crops:

Bajra - *Pennisetum typhoides* Stapf. et Hubbard (Bamboo);
Groundnut - *Arachis hypogaea* L. (Verkkadalai);
Gingelly - *Sessamum indicaum* L. (Ellu);
Cashew nut - *Anacardium occidentale* L (Mundiri)

The main wet crops:

Rice - *Oryza sativa* L. (Nellu)
Ragi - *Eleusine coracana* Gaertn (Kelvaragu)
Sugarcane - *Saccharum officinarum* L (Karumbu);
Bananas - *Musa sp.*; (Valai);
Betel vine - *Piper betel* L. (Vetrilai)

The flora of the region is listed as six categories viz. hygrophytes, plants of halomorphic soils and sand-dunes, plants of sandstones, avenue trees, hedge plants and ornamental plants.

South Arcot Region

The forest of the region may be divided into three main zones that on the Kalrayan hills, the lower Gingee hills and that on the coast. The forest on the kalrayans is of the evergreen type on the highest elevations and in the moist and sheltered ravines and of the deciduous type on the dry and exposed slopes. This deciduous belt extends for a considerable extent eastwards. In the Gingee area mixed forests occur in which the evergreen type preponderates over the deciduous type. On the coast the forest is chiefly evergreen associated with a number of deciduous varieties of trees. The littoral flora is represented by grass spinifex sqarrosus. This plant and another grass, Trachys mucronata, which is also found on the coast, are useful sand-binders. The cultivated plains show the usual Coromandal weeds. Among the shrubs may be mentioned Ehretia buxifolia, Fiueggea leucopyrus Azima tetracantha, Cadaba indica and cassia aurrculata whose bark is largely used for tanning purposes.

2.1.7 Fauna

The fauna of Pondicherry may be taken as essentially the same as that of the nearby districts of Tamil Nadu or Andhra Pradesh, the regions presenting practically the same physical, climatic and biotic features of the surrounding areas. There are four major groups of marine invertebrate fauna commonly met with in the sandy beaches (including Pondicherry) along the coastal line of Bay of Bengal viz. Polychaeta, Crustacea, Mollusea and Echinodermata.

There is nothing remarkable in the fauna of the South Arcot region. The cattle are of inferior breed and are generally fit for the plough only. The Tirukkoyilur and Kallakkurichchi taluks maintain a comparatively large number of cattle is more because grazing land is more common there than elsewhere. Fodder crops are not specially raised in any taluk and the cattle depend chiefly on the straw of cereals.

CHAPTER 3

EARLY HISTORIC SETTLEMENT PATTERN

The study of settlement patterns in archaeology aims at reconstructing the manner in which peoples' cultural activities and social institutions are distributed over the landscape (Rouse 1972). In simple terms it aims at understanding 'why the settlements are situated and where they are?' Settlement approach includes the investigation of three broad systems, viz. cultural, sociological and ecological, with a probe into the possible relationships or interactions amongst them. Of late, this approach has become an integral part of the archaeological research, whose primary concern has been to understand the social, political, cultural and religious and symbolic aspects of ancient cultures that are accessible only in the form of material manifestations.

This chapter contains three sections: (1) origin and development of settlement pattern studies in archaeology, (2) description of the Early Historic sites within the study area and their distribution pattern and (3) site categorization in terms of site function.

3.1 Origin and Development of Settlement Pattern Studies in Archaeology

Settlement pattern studies in Archaeology are a post-World War development. The concept of settlement pattern was originally developed by Julian H. Steward, an ethnographer and has to come to archaeology from the discipline of geography. The pioneering application of this approach in the field of archaeology was made Willey (1955, 1956), in the course of his archaeological investigations in the Viru Valley of Peru. He defines settlement archaeology as the study of the way ancient sites are located where they are and working relationship between people, their environment and technology, man's relationship over the landscape where he lived and the dwelling structures, and considers it "a strategic starting point for the functional interpretation of archaeological cultures, since they reflect the natural environment". The concept of Settlement Archaeology, according to Willey, "does not comprise a self-contained approach to Prehistory.......a 'new archaeology.... But is a 'new approach' within archaeology, which must nevertheless begin with the same factual analytical" (Willey as quoted in Tringham 1972:1).

Chang (1962, 1972) defines settlement pattern Studies as "the manner in which human settlements are arranged over the landscape in relation to the physiographic, geographic environment and community pattern, as the manner in which the inhabitants arrange their various structures within the communities within the aggregate". According to Flannery (1960), "settlement pattern is the study of rules governing the physical arrangement of sites across the landscape". Emphasis has been commonly laid on the study of the relationship between human activities and various micro-and-macro-environments. Settlement pattern studies help particularly in understanding the cultural and social systems of the past. They are also useful in establishing the correlation between civilization and urbanization, in terms of settlement patterns and material remains.

Trigger (1968) defines settlement pattern as "the manner in which people's cultural activities and social institutions are disturbed over the landscape and it is the study of distribution of sites over a given area". The concept of settlement archaeology has been summarized by him as "the study of social relationship using archaeological data", and it provides one of the strongest links between archaeology and ethnography" (Trigger 1963). Trigger (1967) initiated the development of settlement archaeology in a new methodological perspective. He demarcates three different levels of settlement studies in archaeology namely, individual buildings and structures, community level, and zonal pattern. In the first level, emphasis is placed on independent structures and their internal arrangements. The second level i.e., community level, focuses on the arrangement of buildings in a confined locality, highlighting social hierarchy and economic strategies. In such a study, environment and subsistence pattern are taken into account in assessing the size and stability of the community. The third and most important level of settlement study is the zonal pattern, which has a wider geographical perspective covering aspects such as natural resources (water, land, flora and fauna, forest products and such other sources) and their exploitation, economic and ecological adoption of the communities. Studies in India and abroad in settlement archaeology have been mostly based on this approach.

Settlement pattern studies have been carried out in India, especially in the river valleys where sites are generally located. These studies have in general focused on the zonal pattern while analyzing the pattern of the site distribution. In studies involving the prehistoric sites, an ethnographic approach has been adopted to understand the pat human behavior and settlement system (Nanda, 1984 : Ota 1986; Mohanty, 1989; Paddayya, 1993; Pappu, 1995). It is, however, the Proto historic/later prehistoric phase which has attracted the maximum attention with regard to settlement studies (Bhan, 1977; Dhavalikar, 1978; Chitalwala, 1979; Possehl, 1980; Shinde, 1998). In the Early Historic context, research on settlement pattern has been conducted in the Middle Ganga Valley, in the districts of Kanpur (Makkan Lal, 1984) and Alahabad (Erdosy, 1988).

In the present study, the zonal perspective has been adopted for reconstructing the Early Historic Settlement pattern of Arikamedu and its satellite settlements. With this aim, intensive and extensive archaeological fieldwork was carried out in the study are during 2003-2008. The results of which are discussed in the followings. The data collected through the field work has been carefully analyzed and corroborated with available literature on excavations and previous explorations.

The satellite settlements were, in fact, the backbone of the entire trade web, for the urban centers which could never have flourished without them. It appears that the small settlements were specialized in craft activities, extraction of gemstone raw materials and local forest resources which were supplied to the nearby centre. Iron smelting and manufacturing of iron objects constituted another primary occupation.

3.2 Settlements

A distance of about 100 km was explored during five field seasons, along the banks of rivers Gingee, Middle Pennaiyar, Vellar and Manimuka with their major distributaries and tributaries. A total of 14 Early Historic sites were newly discovered, three along the right bank of Pennar, another three along Pombai river, two sites in Gadilam and one each in Gingee and Malattar (Fig.06). 29 sites were re-investigated. Except multiple mounds Tirasu and Karaimedu the vast majority of newly discovered sites are made up of single mound. The surface features at these sites are dominated by potsherds, beads, terracotta objects, occasionally brick architecture are also found. Most of the sites have been subjected to disturbances. These are:-

- Agricultural expansion is one of the causes of site destruction.
- The major natural factor, which disturb site is the floods. Early Historic sites located on the banks of rivers have suffered

damage during past 2000 years. Flood reach has increased during last 200 years and that has augmented large-scale deforestation in the area.

- Expansion of settlements: residential and industrial colonies are on the increase that causes the destruction. For instance, the sites of Manikolai and Karaimedu.

3.2.1 Important Earlier explored & excavated sites in the Study Area

1. Arikamedu

The site of Arikamedu is located on the southeastern coast of India, 4 km south of Pondicherry town, within the Union Territory of Pondicherry. The site is on the right bank of the river Ariyankuppam, at the point where the river joins the Bay of Bengal (Pl. 1-2 and Fig.9). Ariyankuppam is a branch of the river Gingee or Varahanadi that, about 6 km from its mouth, forks into two- the Ariyankuppam to the north and the Chunnambu Aru to the south. Ariyankuppam resembles a brackish lagoon, in which the level of water varies according to the season. During the monsoon season, one could say along the river to the sea in catamaran or even in small motor boats but sand bars often block the passage. Archaeological and historical records, however, indicate that the river was navigable at its mouth till the 18th A.D. The site can be easily reached from Pondicherry town by road.

The site has been identified with the cplace name Poduke cited in the Periplus (80-90 AD?) and the 'Podouke emporion' mentioned by Ptolemy (150 AD). Before the arrival of the French and British in this region, in 16th century AD, Pondicherry town was called Puducheri ('new town' in Tamil), probably a derivation from the Tamil place-name Potikai and Greek Podouke. Very recently, Pondicherry has again been renamed as Puducheri by an act of Parliament.

The site is mentioned in the travel records of a French astronomer, Guillaume Le Gentil who visited Pondicherry in 1768-71 and records that along the high bank of the Ariyankuppam River, diggings had revealed some ten-foot high walls built with large0size bricks. The historical importance of the site and its connection with the Roman Empire was first recognized by Jouveau-Dubreuil, who had started collecting antiquities from the surface of the mound and the river bank as early as 1937. It was excavated for the first time by the Archaeological Survey of India under the direction of Mortimer Wheeler (Wheeler et al., 1946).

Wheeler's excavation divided the site of Arikamedu into two: the Northern Sector and the Southern Sector (Pl. 3 and 4). The Northern Sector was an extension of an area cleared by the earlier French excavators in or after 1941. The Southern Sector had a higher elevation with the mound rising to a height of over 6m above the river level. The Northern Sector revealed a brick structure covering over 50m land identified as a ware house along with a ring well (Pl.5 and 6). The Southern Sector revealed two tanks that may have been used as dyeing vats along with other structures (Pl. 7-8 and Fig.9, 13).

The pottery finds from the digs included both imported and local varieties. Among the imported pottery were fragments of the terra sigillata and amphora jars of ancient times and Chinese Celadon pottery of a later period, mainly tenth-twelfth centuries AD. The excavators presumed that many of the Rouletted pottery (Pl.9) specimens were imports but later studies have firmly indicated that this was a local variety inspired by the Mediterranean pottery. Besides, inscriptions in Tamil Brahmi have been found engraved in many of the potsherds at Arikamedu (Pl.10).

The digs revealed over two hundred beads made of various materials like terracotta, glass, shell, bone, gold and semiprecious stones such as agate, carnelian and amethyst (Pl.11-13). The occurrence of unfinished beads and bits of semi-precious stones indicated the existence of a lapidary at the site. Other finds from the site included fragments of Roman glass bowls, broken mud lamp, a group of terracotta human figurines, iron nails and blade, a copper rattle, an ornamented ivory rod, conch shell ear ornaments and bangles and the wooden leg of a cot or a stool. Of the numerous pieces of rope, the longest had a length of about nine inches and a diameter of about one inch. It was made of three strands of coconut fibers twisted together. Among the stone objects were four pestles and a grinding-stone. Various stones such as granite, sandstone and steatite were used for making these objects. Three coins were unearthed- two of them were corroded beyond identification; the third one belonged to the reign of the king Raja Raja I (985-1014 AD) of the Chola dynasty. On the basis of the excavated materials, Wheeler concluded that Arikamedi was an Indo-Roman trading station that flourished during the first two centuries AD. According to him, the Chinese Celadon pottery and the Chola coin of a later period clearly relate, not to the occupation of the site, but for its destructions during the medieval period.

A full report of Wheeler's excavation was published in Ancient India No.2 (1946). A noteworthy contribution of the excavation was the preparation of a contour map of the site and the surrounding area. This was one of the first large scale archaeological excavations in the while of South India. The excavation received wide publicity throughout India and it soon emerged as a model for its methodology. Throughout the digs at Arikamedi, Wheeler taught his principle of Stratigraphy-based excavations to the students. Another interesting but little-known fact is that it was Wheeler who vigorously popularized the name 'Arikamedu' for the place, although this name was not known prior to his time. The earlier French scholars generally referred to the place as Virampattinam. In fact, the first article written by Wheeler (1944), drawing attention to this site, bore the title "Virampatnam". Following Arikamedu excavation, Wheeler intensified his research on the maritime trade between Rome and South India.

Arikamedu was excavated again in between 1947 and 1950 by the French archaeologist J M Casal (Casal, 1949). He excavated a very large area, spread over three excavation seasons. His excavation revealed that the site extended at least 420m north-south along the river while the width was about 200m east-west in the Northern Sector and 100m or more in the Southern Sector. Many of the artifacts collected from his digs are comparable to those of Wheeler. However, Casal was the first to recognize Iron Age levels in the Stratigraphy. But unlike Wheeler's excavation, Casal's digs went almost unnoticed and till recently, the latter's writings were rarely cited. There are many reasons for this. First Casal's excavations were never fully published; they were partially published by him in 1949 and again, in 1956. Both these publications are in French and hence, were not available to the non-French scholars.

After a comprehensive review of archaeological work at Arikamedu Vimala Begley carried out further excavation during 1989-92, supported by a joint India-American team. The excavation was formally christened as Arikamedu Excavation Project. The basic objectives of this excavation were to better understand the nature of maritime commerce between ancient South India and the Mediterranean region and also learn more about an early Indian port town-how it functioned and what sustained its economy. The excavation spanned three seasons-1989-90, 1990-91 and 1991-92. It adopted the latest sophisticated methods hitherto unknown to either Indian archaeologists or to Indian Archaeology. It, however, retained the earlier division of the site into Northern and Southern Sectors (Fig. 22). Simultaneously, the Arikamedu Excavation protect attempted a re-examination and reassessment of the finds from the earlier - work of Wheeler and Casal at the site. The results of these digs and researches have been published in to sumptuous volumes (Begley et al., 1996 and 2004).

Results of these excavations clearly revealed that Arikamedu was not only fashioned by the minds of Romans, but was at the heart of Megalithic Culture. As per the latest archaeological evidence, the site was first occupied around the late 3rd century or early 2nd century BC. This period belongs to the late Iron Age or Megalithic Age in South

India. The earliest habitation was in the Southern Sector and not in the Northern Sector. Fishing and head-making were important occupations of this community.

Karaikadu

Karaikudu, also called Kudikadu and Nattamedu, is a coastal site over 30 Km south of Arikamedu. Karaikadu lies at the backwaters (uppanar) which could provide the necessary shelter for the anchorage of boats. The Archaeological Survey of India excavated the site in 1966. At that time, the area had extensive plantations and hence, the land available for excavation was very limited. After the clearance of the plantations, the Department of Ancient History and Archaeology of the University of Madras conducted further digs at the site in 1989. The finds from Karaikadu, specially the locally-made and imported pottery, are strikingly similar to those reported from Arikamedu. For example, like Arikamedu, Karaikadu too revealed bricks, conch shell artifacts, Roman style Rouletted pottery, fragments of imported amphora jars, and conical jars modeled on the amphora jars. The other finds from Karaikadu include terracotta pipes, crucibles and waste slag used in the manufacture of glass. The site has yielded glass and semi-precious stone beads at various stages of manufacture. Some of the glass beads from Karaikadu are so similar to those from Arikamedu that it has been remarked that these beads might have been made in Arikamedu and sent to Karaikadu. A brick structure associated with the head-making industry was also underthed at Karaikadu. All these finds have been dated to around the 1st century AD. Like Arikamedu, Karaikadu has evidences of human habitation up to the medieval times. In view comparable finds and close spatial proximity to Arikamedu, archaeologists sometimes regard Karaikadu as an extension of Arikamedu.

In the 1990s, modern factory buildings have sprung up on the ancient stie of Karaikadu. Some of the artifacts recovered during this construction are now in the small Government Museum at Cuddalore (Tamil Nadu).

Tirukoilur

Tirukoilur, earlier called Koval or Kovalur, is now a small town located on the south bank of the river Thenpennar (or south Pennar). The place has many Hindu temples built during different periods.

During the period of the Roman trade, Tirukoilur was the capital of the Malaiyaman chieftains. They exercised control over Malaiyaman Nadu which inclided parts of the present-day Pondicherry and the adjoining South Arcot region of Tamil Nadu. The Malaiyaman rulers were very powerful. Malaiyaman Tirumudi Kari was one of the most famous rulers of this dynasty. It is locally believed that the port of Arikamedu was under their control for some years.

Tirukoilur has revealed hundreds of quadrangular copper coins minted by the Malaiyamans. One face of the most of these coins exhibits hillocks, road and river. According to art historians, these motifs may together represent the physical topography of the Malaiyaman chiefdom, particularly their capital Tirukoilur. The hills on the coins together represent the physical topography of the Malaiyaman chiefdom, particularly their capital Tirukoilur. The hills on the coins may denote the Muller hills that were part of the Malaiyaman territory. The river on the coins may be the South Pennar on whose bank Tirukoilur is situated. When the river reaches Tirukoilur from the hills, it takes a sharp bend that has been clearly shown on the most of the coins. Close to this bend, there is a rocky outcrop which may be the mound appearing on the coins. The road seen on the coins may be one of the ancient highways that connected Tirukoilur with other trade centers such as Arikamedu, Kanchipuram, Karur and Uraiyur. Significantly, in ancient South India, the highway often ran parallel to the river. Tirukoilur has also yielded Roman gold and copper coins ranging from the 1st to the 3rd-4th centuries AD.

The Tamil Nadu state Department of Archaeology conducted excavations at Tirukoilur in the year 1994. Due to modern constructions, it was very difficult to find vacant sites for the excavations. Hence, the digs had to be conducted in places such as a temple and school playground. The excavations revealed three cultural periods based on the artifacts unearthed at the site. These are period I (100 BC-400 AD); Period II (400 AD-1300 AD) and Period III (1300-1700 AD).

Period I (100 BC to 400 AD) at the site represents the Megalithic culture and evidence for Roman trade. The period has yielded glass beads, the Roman Style Rouletted Pottery and a unique amphora jar fragment - all objects similar to those found at Arikamedu. The Tirukoilur amphora fragment is from the body portion of the jar. Pale pink in colour, the shred is cdevoid of any slip or incrustation. Besides, theer is a unique inscription on a cave in the hill to the east of a neighbouring village named Jambai on the north bank of the South Pennar. The inscription is in the Tamil Language and the Tamil Brahmi script. It belongs to the 1st century AD. It records the gift of the cave shelter by a local chieftian.

Suttukeni

Suttukeni or Soutoukeny is situated on the banks of the river Gingee in the Union Territory of Pondicherry. It is an important Megalithic settlement that was excavated in 1950 by a team of French archaeologists headed by J. M. Casal. As Arikamedu is situated, around 30 Kms away from Suttukeni, closer to the sea, on the banks of the river Ariyankuppam, a branch of the Gingee there is a strong suspicion that both these sites may have had commercial and cultural contacts through the reverine route. Both the sites share several common features. The Megalithic burials at Suttukeni are almost contemporary with the earliest settlement at Arikamedu (3rd-2nd cent. BC). Some of the typical megalithic potteries found at Suttukeni are identical to those reported from Arikamedu.

Suttukeni has yielded a fragmentary bronze vessel that appears to be an import from the Mediterranean region. If so, the vessel would have reached the site vide Arikamedu. The Megalithic grave at Suttukeni revealed several specimens of gold jewellery including decorated gold spacers probably intended for four-strand necklaces (Pl.14). A similar four-holed separator but without any decoration has been discovered at Arikamedu. Further, many of the beads found at Suttukeni are similar to those reported from Arikamedu (see Pl.12-13).

Sengamedu

This site is situated at a distance of 80 Kms southwest of Arikamedu, Sengamedu is a very extensive site, nearly 26 acres in area, perched on the left bank of the river Manimuktar, a tributary of river Vellar (Pl.15). The site is about 23 Kms from Vriddhachalam town in Villupuram District. The site has the unique distinction of being one of the earliest Megalithic habitation sites to be excavated in Tamil Nadu. The excavations were conducted by the ASI in the early 1950s.

A unicultural site in nature, the chronology of Sengamedu on the basis of the cultural material has been designated to Pre-Rouletted, Rouletted and post Rouletted roughly ranging from 300 BC-200 AD. The occupation of the site (period I) begins with the Black and Red ware of the Iron Age. Period II (post-Megalithic, roughly around first century AD) of the site has revealed the Roman style Rouletted pottery resembling the ones from Arikamedu. The most important finds from the Sengamedu are the ruins of ancient brick structures spread over a large area at least 20 m long and 5 m wide. Indeed, the very name 'Sengamedu' is believed to have been derived from the Tamil words 'Sengal medu' meaning 'mound of bricks' (Pl.16 and 17). These ruins, like those at Arikamedu, lie right on the river bank. The size (30 cms × 18 cms × 7.6 cms) of the Sengamedu bricks is almost the same at that of the bricks of the Roman period bricks at Arikamedu. Like Arikamedu, Sengamedu has also revealed ring wells, terracotta figurines, mud lamps and a large number of beads. Hence, the excavators of this site are tempted to suspect that Arikamedu and Sengamedu had commercial links through riverine routes. But the precise details of these links await further investigations.

Sendamanglam

This historical site lies 1 Km east of the NH No. 42a. This once served as the capital of Kadava king Koperusinganan. In the inscription this place mentioned as Sendamanglam. The site was excavated in the year 1995 and 1996 by the State Archaeology Department. The site yielded a brick structure, a conical jar, a bronze seal, rouletted ware, terracotta figurines and medieval times (Rajan 1997).

Tiruvamattur

The site lies on the river Pambaiyar and 5 kms northwest of Villupuram. According to the local legend, the village named after the hornless cattle got its horn by praying god Shiva. The habitation mound on the bank of the river on the southern side of the village was excavated in the year 1987-88 by the Department of Ancient History and Archaeology, University of Madras. Three trenches were laid. It yielded Black and Red ware, Red polished ware, Rouletted ware, graffiti marks, terracotta figurines, lamps, stone beads and bangles (Rajan 1997).

Kurur

This habitation-cum-burial site is on the Kallakurichi-Kuttakudi road at a distance of 9 kms from Kallakurichchi. There are two habitation mounds. The habitation mound with Iron Age cultural deposit called nattamodu is found on the southern side of the village in the field called mudikondan. This mound yielded black and red ware of thin variety. The historical habitation mound covering an area of more than 15 acres found near the village Ramanathapuram. Bricks, terracotta lamps, coarse red ware and beads were collected. There is a Siva temple nearby. An urn burial site found on the left bank of river Gomuki is in the field locally called Kuppaimodu (Rajan 1997).

Niraimathi

It lies on the Kallakurichchi-Kuttakudi road at a distance of 9 kms from Kallakurichchi. Historical habitation mound covering an area of more than 10 acres found on the bank of river Gomuki yielded red ware, tiles, brick bats and terracotta beads.

Ring wells are noticed on the bank of Gomuki probably used for agriculture (Rajan 1997).

Palayapattinam

Palayapattinam lays 10 kms from Vridhachchalam and 3 kms from Virdhachchalam-Ulundurpettai road passing through the village Virareddiyur.

The habitation mound covering an area of more than 10 acres lies near the village. The surface collection include terracotta beads, tiles, brick pieces in addition with usual BRW, BSW and RW suggested that the site would have existed till historical period. The mound is locally known as niralaimodu. The urn burial site lies opposite to the habitation (Rajan 1997).

Maligaimedu

This site is located in Panruti taluk of Cuddalore district. The site was excavated by the State Department of Archaeology, Tamil Nadu Government in the year 1999-2000. Three cultural sequences have been exposed from the excavation. The excavation has yielded black and red ware, red ware, black ware, Rouletted ware, coarse red ware, inscribed potteries and a copper coin with the Ujjain symbol. According to the excavator the habitation at the site starts from c. 3rd century BC (from State Archaeology web site).

Newly Explored Sites

As mentioned earlier during the course of field work in the study area, a total number of 14 Early Historic sites were discovered, 3 along the right bank of Pennar, another 3 along Pombai reiver, 2 sites in Gadilam and 2 each in Gingee & Malattar. A description of the sites is in the following:-

Kottaimedu

This Early Historical site is located in Puranasingapalayam village which is located 4 Kms north of Tibhuvani (once a great Chola town), which is situated about 27 Kms. West of Pondicherrry towards Villupuram. The village Puranasingapalayam, is located 20 Kms west of Arikamedu. In the vicinity of Puranasingapalayam, the pottery and debris-bearing deposits rise to 5 m meters above the dry river bed of the Pambai (Pl. 18). The very name Kottaimedu reminds us that there once a fort (kottai), which in later years collapsed (Pl. 19-20), and the debris of the collapsed fort walls then formed a Mound (medu).

The site, as it stands today, has suffered considerable damage from a variety of factors, particularly agricultural expansion. Indeed, the site is approximately 8 to 10 acres, and is now widely used for cultivation of both irrigated and non-irrigated crops such as paddy, egg plant (brinjal), tomato, flowers, coconuts and bananas.

Artifacts collected from the site include an amphora and Rouletted ware, together with those of white slipped bowls and dishes, the bluntly pointed base of a large storage jar and top, body and lower fragments of tall conical vessel tapering town to a point at the base. In addition, two beads and a glass object were also discovered on the surface.

The ceramic types are typical of the Early Historic period. The forms and fabic have a very high similarity with that of Arikamedu's classical trade phases (Fig. 23 and Pl. 21-22).

Ring Well

A terracotta ring well has been discovered a few meters east of a new bridge under construction on the river Pambai in the vicinity of Puranasingapalayam, Five rings have been noticed in a section at the site. The top and bottom of the ringwell are uncertain; presently two top rings are damaged. The diameter of the third visible ring is about one meter and the height of each ring is about 30 cms. this type of ring well was discovered in Arikamedu and contemporary sites.

Tirasu

Tirasu (Long: 79° 34'N : Lat 11° 48' E) is located in Panruti taluk of Cuddalore district (Pl.23). It is situated 22 Kms southest of Villupuram and on the right bank river Pennar. Adjacent to this site excavated site Maligaimedu is located. Here a mound has been identified in the form of cultivation ground. The height of the mound varies from 50 Cms ot 1 meter. During the course of exploration few ancient bricks (Pl.24 and 25), potsherds of coarse red ware, fine red ware and black and red ware have been found. Graffiti is also observed on some potsherds. Other antiquities include shell bangle, brick bats, terracotta figurines and hopscotch. On the basis of material evidence this site is assigned to Early Historical period and match with Arikamedu chronology.

Karaimedu

Karaimedu (Long: 79° 37' N; Lat: 11° 48' E) is about 15 kms from Villupuram on Villupuram-Pondicherry road. A huge mound lies close to the local pond. The height of the mound varies from 2 to 3 m (Pl.26). Here some years ago villagers had dug the mound in order to provide a pathway on the pond. This had brought to light many ring well (Pl.27). During the course of present exploration on the advice of the villagers and trench measuring 1 × 1 m was dug, where larger rim portions of ring wells were unearthed. After documenting the surface carefully at a depth of about 7-10 cm a broken ring came to surface. At a depth of about 1.5 m a total number of found rings were found (Pl.28 and 29). As mentioned by the villagers here too broken dish and some bone fragments were also found from the bottom level (Plate XI). The rings were red in colour and approximate dia of each ring measures 80 cms. From the excavation it is inferred that originally the rings were prepared for storing/getting potable water later when the rings were not in use they were either for burial purpose or for as dust bins.

Arakandanallur

Arakandanallur (Long: 79° 14' N; Lat: 11° 58' E) lies opposite to Tirukkoyilur on the northern bank of river Pennar (Pl.30), The incomplete rock-cut temple, facing due east, is cut on the eastern scrap of the large rock, on the top of which stands the gopuram and the stone enclosure of the Opporuvarumillada Nayanar and Ponniyamman temples. Ponniyamman was perhaps a Jaina goddess Jvalamalani and Ponniyakki.

During the course of present survey large bricks wer found in the northern bank of river Pennar (Pl.31 and 32). The bricks were found scattered in haphazard manner. The size 30 × 18 × 7.6 cms) of the Arakandanallur bricks is almost the same as that of the bricks of the Roman period at Arikamedu. The exact purpose of these bricks could not be ascertained because the floods had submerged thc area. When enquiring the local people who frequently use to come to river for bath and fishing informed that whenever the river is dry they happened to see a huge brick structure in the northern bed of the river. Further proper excavation in the river banks may prove the importance of the so called structure.

Kottapakkatuveli

This village Kottapakkatuveli (Long: 79° 30' N; Lat: 11° 57' E) is located 2 kms away from Villupuram town (Pl.33). Adjacent to this site the dry bed of river Pombai (a tributary of river Pennar) is visible. Hence during the course of exploration large size bricks and terracotta figurines were found. The brick size is of the standard 30 × 18 × 7.6 cms of the Roman period bricks at Arikamedu. A few Terracotta figurines have also recovered.

Manikolai

This site Manikolai (Long: 79° 42' N; Lat: 11° 30' E) is located about 30 kms Cuddalore town (near Ottathai village) on Cuddalore to Chidambaram road. During the exploration potsherds of black and red ware, coarse red ware, fine red ware and grey ware found from a cultivation field, which is located opposite to Modern CSI church. Besides potsherds, large number of glass beads along with rough outs were collected from the same locality (Pl.34). The glass beads in different shapes and variable colors mainly include dark blue, dull red, black, violet, green and yellow shows similarity with Arikamedu bead discoveries. The approximate area of site is 2 ha.

Thirusopuram

The site Thirusopuram (Long: 79° 45' N; Lat 11° 35' E) is located about 15 kms east of Cuddalore town (after crossing Pondiyampakkam railway station) on Cuddalore to Chidambaram road. River Uppanar flows near the site (Pl.35). This place along with adjacent village Thiyagavalli (named after Kulothunga Cholan's wife) was part of Chaturvedi Mangalam in later Chola period (c. 12th – 13th Cent. AD). A temple dedicated to Shive with a Late Chols inscriptions attest the Chola antiquity of the village. Here along the seashore area, during exploration, a mound locally known as chalimedu (i.e. mound with full of potsherds) is located. The site has yielded humpty a numbers of potsherds of black and red ware, coarse red ware, fine red ware and grey ware (Pl.36). Further intensive survey in the same area yielded good numbr of glass beads (Pl.37).

The glass beads in different shapes and variable colors mainly include dark blue, dull red, black, violet, green and yellow shows similarity with Arikamedu bead collections (Pl.38). According to local historian this place Thirusopuram is nothing but ancient sopatana mentioned by western geographers.

In this context, the recent excavation (2005-06) conducted by State Department of Archaeology, Tamil Nadu Government at Marakkanam, a site located about 35 kms from Tindivanam in Villupuram district (which is supposed to be believed as ancient sopatna) did not yield any artifacts beyond Medieval period. Even the local historian further informed that about a decade he had found base of conical jar (amphora?) from the same site. But the same has not lost recently. Whereas the meaning of the term "Sopuram" indicates that Fort. It may be inferred that from the name Sopuram that the place was a fortified town. Adjacent to this mound a small stream known as uppanar flows into sea. Further thorough exploration/excavation may attest the antiquity of this site and comparison of this to ancient sopatana.

Smallar Sites

Besides above mentioned newly discovered sites, some less important sites but significant once with Early Historical vestiges were also discovered during the present survey. They are likely contemporary with Arikamedu and details of them are mentioned below:-

Thirunavalur

Thirunavalue (Long: 79° 24'N; Lat: 11° 45'E) is located 34 kms south of Cuddalore town and it is situated on the right bank of Gadilam river. During the exploration Coarse Red Ware, red ware and Black and Red Ware sherds were found. Besides this, one terracotta human figurine was also found.

Kattuselur

Kattuselur (Long: 79° 10'N; Lat: 11° 50'E) is located about 50 Kms north of Villupuram town and 15 kms east of Tirukoilur. It is situated on the right bank of Kadilam River. During the exploration coarse red ware, red ware and Black & red ware sherds were found. One terracotta figurine was also found.

Terracotta Lamps

During the exploration Terracotta lamkps with many sides found from three sites viz. Arasur (Long: 79° 14'N; Lat: 11° 58'E) (located on the right bank of river Malatar), Sendiyambakkam (Long: 79° 18'N; Lat: 11° 59'E)(located on the left bank of river Sankarabarani) and Siruvalai (Long: 79° 25'N; Lat:12° 00'E) (located 16 kms east of Villupuram).

Smoking Pipes

Further during the exploration Terracotta smoking pipes were discovered from Karaimedu, Kottapakkatuveli, Arasur and Parikal (Long: 79° 22'N; Lat: 11° 47'E) along with early historical potsherds.

3.2.2 The Distribution of Archaeological Sites in the Study Region

Pondicherry Region

The distribution pattern of Iron Age cemetery sites in the Pondicherry area and its immediate neighborhood shows that they are concentrated mainly on the northern area of the Gingee River (Fig.16). A few cemetery sites have been discovered on the southern area of the Gingee River. These are basically urn burials and the burial urns are placed in pits cut in to the red soil. The pits are occasionally marked by a stone circle. Less often, sarcophagi have been placed in a chamber of granite slabs placed in a swastika pattern (Pl.39) and Suthukeni and Auroville (Pl.40) around Pondicherry. Urn burials found at Perambai and Mutharapalaeom are without any surface marking.

Urn burials have also been identified in alluvial deposits of the Gingee river, at Purangkuppam and Sorappattu. An urn burial was dug out at Bahour by local historian by name Kuppuswamy (Kuppusamy, 'Funeral urns of Bahour' in Review Historic de-la Pondicherry, Vol. 12 Pondicherry: 1974-75, Pp 1-10).

The distribution of Iron Age burials in the Pondicherry area seems much more complicated. Both the cist and urn burials are found together in the same region. Due to this I have classified the Pondicherry area into three regions on the basis of Geological formations and same as follows:-

Zone A-Area covered by Cuddalore formation.

Zone B-Area covered by Upper Cretaceous and Palaeocene formations.

Zone-C-Area covered by fluvial deposits.

Zone A

The upper tertiary sediments of the Pondicherry region is represented by the Cuddalore formation, which occurs as two widely separated outcrops: one on the north-eastern margin, just along the northern coast of Pondicherry (Pl.41). Interestingly a great density of Iron age burials are noticed in this zone.

Main Sites: Auroville, Thiruvakarai and Suthukeni. These sites are having both urn burials and Cist burials.

Typology of Iron Age Burial

Typologically the Iron Age burials in the Pondicherry area are not different from those of Tamil Nadu.

Zone B

It lies between the Cuddalore Formation on the east and to the west of the Gingee River. It is a combination of Vanur sand stone, ottai clay stone and Turuvai limestone of Upper Cretaceous period of Kadaperi and Manveli Formation of Palaeocene period.

There are no known archaeological sites in this zone.

Zone C

Three-fourth of the Pondicherry area is covered by quaternary fluvial deposits, largely alluvium (Pl.42). The thickness of this alluvium varies from 10.5 to 0.5 m. At Sathamanglam it is about 0.55 m. Zone C is mostly undr cultivation because of this alluvium deposit.

Important Sites: Soarppattu, Puranagkuppam, Nattamedu and Bahour.

Soarappattu

It is located in the doab of Gingee and Pambai rivers. The site is under cultivation, although a few body shreds and rims of urns, black and red ware, red ware, black ware are found in the ploughed field. But as of today no site in this region has the evidence for megalithic burials.

Puranagkuppam

It is located on the south bank (of the South Outlet) of the Gingee River and another site known as Nattamedu is located between Gingee and South Pennar.

Therefore, Zone-C is only noted for urn burials and no evidence of cist burials have been reported from this region so far.

South Arcot Region

In 1876 J.H. Garstin made the first discoveries of megalithic at Kollur and Devanur (Garstin 1876). Since then explorations carried out over the years, have revealed a number of megaliths all over the region. About 175 archaeological sites have been recorded of which 143 are megalithic and remaining are Early Historic. Among the burial sites, 24 are cairn circles, 11 are with stone circles, 1 dolmenoid cist, 86 urn burials and 12 sarcophagi sites (Fig.16). Each type of distributed with in a specific geographical zone of this region (Rajan 1998).

Spatial Distributional Pattern of Megalithic Burials

In the South Arcot region there is a dominance of three distinct megalithic types, confined to three separate geographical zones. The first, cairn circle category is mainly concentrated in the hilly tracts. The stone circles without any cairn packing are also seen. The second type – the urn burials are noticed in the eastern part of the region particularly to the south of the river Pennar, widespread in the deltaic area of the rivers Kaveri and Vellar. The third variety, consisting of sarcophagus burials are mainly found to north of the Pennar River in the non-deltaic region of this district. In some parts of the study area these three categories overlap. The concentrations of cairn circles enclosing a cist with a round porthole on the east are found in great density in the western part of this region, particularly in the Kallakurichchi and tirukkoyilur taluks. This area is drained by the rivers Pennar, Vellar and Gomuki. The distribution of cairn circles with cists in concentrated in the zone between 200-500 AMSL. Once the river reaches the plain (below 200 AMSL) the density of cairn circles decreases drastically. The area covered by the talukas of Kattumannar koil, Chidambaram, Cuddalore, Panruti, Tidivanam, Virdhachalam and the eastern part of Tittakudi, all of which occupy the eastern part of this region, is devoid of megalithic sites of any category.

Stone circles, which are degenerate forms of the cairn circle, are found to the north of Varahanadi (Tindivanam and Gingee tluks). These stone circles invariably contained within them an urn or sarcophagus depending on the external context.

Early Historical Phase

In the old South Arcot Region (Villupuram and Cuddalore), the Early Historic period is marked by the emergence of brick structure, ring wells, terracotta lamps, beads, Rouletted Ware, punch-marked coins, Roman coins and coins of Malayaman (the Sangam Age chieftain),, Tamil-Brahmi inscriptions from Jain beds (Fig.20). There are 26 sites as shown in the following Table.

Table 1: Important Early Historical Sites in South Arcot Region

S. No.	Name	Taluk	District	Nature of the Site
1.	Nekanurpatti	Gingee	Villupuram	Tamil-Brahmi Inscription, rock painting
2.	Perumpugai	Gingee	Villupuram	Jain beds on hillock.
3.	Thondur	Gingee	Villupuram	Tamil-Brahmi inscription, Jain beds.
4.	Kurur	Kallakurichi	Villupuram	Bricks, T.C. lamps & beads.
5.	Niraimathi	Kallakurichi	Villupuram	Tiles, brickbats, T.C. beads and ring wells.
6.	Peral	Kallakurichi	Villupuram	Historical mound.
7.	Siruvallur	Kallakurichi	Villupuram	Crucible fragments.
8.	Perumukkal	Tindivanam	Villupuram	Rock engraving.
9.	Tiruvakkarai	Tindivanam	Villupuram	Coral bead & Glass bead.
10.	Adichchanur	Tirukkoyilur	Villupuram	Silver Punch marked coins.
11.	Arakandanallur	Tirukkoyilur	Villupuram	Jain centre.
12.	Jambai	Tirukkoyilur	Villupuram	Athiyaman inscription.
13.	Kiranur	Tirukkoyilur	Villupuram	Jain beds.
14.	Kottakam	Tirukkoyilur	Villupuram	193 Roman coins of C. 3rd century AD.

contd....

S. No.	Name	Taluk	District	Nature of the Site
15.	Thotti	Tirukkoyilur	Villupuram	14 Jain beds.
16.	Tirukkoyilur	Tirukkoyilur	Villupuram	Rouletted ware & Terracotta beads.
17.	Virapandi	Tirukkoyilur	Villupuram	Iron slag.
18.	Tholudur	Tittakudi	Villupuram	Historical habitation mound.
19.	Sendamanglam	Ulundurpettai	Villupuram	Brick structure, conical jar, a bronze seal, Rouletted ware & Terracotta figurine.
20.	Kalpattu	Villupuram	Villupuram	Jain bed.
21.	Karuvakshi	Villupuram	Villupuram	Rouletted ware, Graffiti, Terracotta figurine, lamps, stone beads & bangles.
22.	Iranji	Virudhachchalam	Cuddalore	Terracotta beads.
23.	Sengamedu	Virudhachchalam	Cuddalore	Rouletted ware, Graffiti, Terracotta figurine, lamps.
24.	Palayapattinam	Virudhachchalam	Cuddalore	Terracotta beads, tiles & brick pieces.
25.	Karaikadu	Cuddalore	Cuddalore	Rouletted ware, conical jar, beads.
26.	Kudikadu	Cuddalore	Cuddalore	Floor level & beads.

(After Rajan 1997: 324-334)

3.3 Site Categorization

The Early Historic sites in the study region comprise a few large settlements (centers) and several small settlements (Satellites) which are located in the proximity of large settlements. On the basis of area of occupation, habitation deposit and material remains, it may be suggested that the sites of Arikamedu, Kudikadu, Manikollai and Thirusopuram are functioned as central places. These sites are situated in strategic locations, and by virtue of their location controlled the dynamics of inter-and intra regional trade.

Here these four sites served as trade centers where iron (as raw material/finished products), terracotta objects, previous and semi-precious gemstones, molluses and forest products (timber, bamboo, herbs and medical plants) were brought in from satellite sites, and traded.

The satellite settlements were, in fact, the backbone of the whole trade network, for the urban centers could never flourished without them. It appears that the small settlements were specialized in craft activities, extraction of gemstones and local forest resources.

3.4 Centre – Periphery Relationship

A study of the relationship between Centres – Periphery is a Post-war development. It developed as a capitalistic approach was the relationship of urban market system or industrial setups with rural settlements were analyzed (Wallerstein 1974). The Centre – Periphery model has figured in a variety of ways in the geographical analysis of the spatial organization of human cultures and societies. According to Champion (1989: 2), the main intention of the centre-periphery model is to explore a particular alternative framework- the analysis of long distance relationship, especially between societies with markedly different patterns of social or economic organization and the potential of such argument interactions to bring about major transformations of social relations. The demarcation of such type of long distance relationship may be drawn with the concepts such as 'diffusion', 'influence' and 'trade'.

This perspective has been adopted in the present study, while dealing with the relationship between urban and satellite settlements and relationships between and among them in a defined geographical area. As noted above, the small settlements in the study region show a tendency to converge around the larger centers. These smaller settlements were rich in diverse economic resources with opportunities for diversifying human activities and occupation such as extraction of gemstones and forest resources, weaving, terracotta art and pottery making. Material products were supplied to the nearby centers, from where these were transported to distant settlements. This interaction consequently led to integration of resource areas with production and distribution areas.

3.5 Early Historic Urbanization in Tamil Nadu

Early Historic

The term 'Early Historic' is defined as a chronological unit spanning the period from c. 300 BC to 500 AD. The Early Historic period in Tamil Nadu has been variously known as 'Sangam Age', 'Megalithic' and 'Indo-Roman period', though there is no discernible variation in the character of culture (Gurukkal 1989). 'Megalithic' is not treated as a distinct chronological period, but a burial tradition that is more frequently associated with the Iron Age continuous into later period (Fig. 21). The Early Historic period may be divided into phase I (pre-1st century BC), and Phase II, (1st century BC to 3rd century AD), coinciding with the 'Indo-Roman', or Indian Ocean trade, and Phase III (post-3rd -6th century to 500 AD), the post-Sangam Age, with each of these phases witnessed distinct levels of development (Selvakumar 2008).

3.5.1 Urbanizm and Unbanization

Urbanism and Urbanization have been the focus of geographical, anthropological and historical studies (Weber, 1992; Wirth, 1938; Childe, 1950; Mumford, 1961; Rapport and Overing 2000: 374-380). Gorden Childe was the first to define urbanization in the context of social evolution and distinguished it by craft specialization, emergence of political economy which did not involve subsistence related activities; generation of social surplus through taxes or tribute; presence of monumental public buildings; use of a writing system; increase in long distance trade; and the dominance of the social elite (Childe 1950). Childe's ten criteria on urbanization have been a subject of discussion among several scholars (Venkatasubramanian 1988; Parasher-Sen 1989: 124). Wirth (1938) defined city as 'a relatively large, dense, permanent settlement of socially heterogeneous individuals'. According to Sjoberg (1960), pre-Industrial cities were characterized by government, religious centers and literate elites rather than dense concentration of population focused on manufacturing and commercial activities.

Urbanization is a process that leads to the emergence and sustenance of cities, which are differentiated by higher population density, large scale commercial and manufacturing activities, among other characteristic (Carter, 1983; Fields, 1999). Cities are to be viewed as an integral part of the society rather than separate entities (Weber, 1922). Hence, the recent urban studies focus on the processes (substance) that influenced the entire society rather than cities (forms) (A1-Zubaidi, n.d).

3.5.2 Current Theories on Urbanization in Ancient Tamilakam

The Harappan civilization is considered to represent the first urbanization in South Asia. The emergence of cities particularly in the Ganga valley, in the pre-Maurayan-Maurayan period is considered second urbanization (Lal 1984; Thaper 1984; Erdosy 1988; Chakrabarti

1988' 1999; Sharma 1994; Allchin 1995). The subject of Early Historic urbanization in Tamil Nadu has received considerable attention from scholars. There have been a series of debates on the dynamics and processes of urbanization in Tamilakam. This second urbanization spread all over South Asia through political expansion and trade control (Selvakumar 2008). These deliberations have centered on the internal dynamics, e.g., growth and interaction among the micro regions within the Tamil country, and external dynamic such as migration of people, ideas and artifacts from North India and trade contacts with the outside regions(Begley 1986; Champakalakshmi 1996; Venkatasubramanian 1996; Gurukkal 1998).

Champakalakshmi (1975-76; 1996:9) contends that urban forms of ancient Tamilakam did not result from internal growth. It manifested as a 'secondary generation' triggered by inter-regional trade over a widespread region including the nearest neighbour Andhra Pradesh and the distant Ganga valley. Maritime trade with the Mediterranean region was also very effective. In her view, there was not state society in the Early Historic Tamil region and it was largely 'tribal' in nature (Chambakalakshmi 1996: 16). She also emphasizes that Mauryan influence was minimal in the Tamil country and that the impact of overseas trade was higher.

Gurukkal (1989,1995), while discussing socio-economic formations in the Tamilakam, contends that ancient Tamil society was in a 'tribal stage', where relationships of productions were kinship-based and the political formations were at chiefdom level, not representing the 'early stage'. He highlights the role of Mauryan contacts on Tamilkam (Gurukkal, 1998), and argues that state formation took place during Early Medieval period when orthodox religions and wet agriculture took firm roots in the Tamil region.

Seneviratne (1993) lays emphasis on the coalescence of internal and external factors in the emergence of early political economics (and urbanization) in Tamilakam. Giving primacy to the role of internal dynamics, he argues that the interactions among micro zones led to the integration of smaller settlements (kudi) into macro eco-zones (nadu), and the formation of 'areas of attractions' in the coastal deltaic plains due to the internal developments.

Morrison (1997) in her synthesis of the Early Historic period argues that the urbanism in South India had an indigenous growth. She states that the interpretations of the distribution of NBPW can also be seen as uncritical archaeological transformations of arguments by historians about the primary of the Gangetic plain as an exporter of 'civilization' to central and southern India, arguments that range from a notion of simple cultural and political 'influence' to outright control (Morrison 1997: 94).

Rajan (2001) on the other hand argues that the early states of Tamilakam were well known in the 3rd century BC and the antecedents would certainly date back to 500 BC. This argument is based on the fact that if the southern kingdoms were a force to reckon with compelling Ashoka Maurya to remain on their northern frontiers.

Ray (2002) is of the view that there must have been some local developments that led to urbanization in the peninsula India from its moorings in Mediterranean trade on the one hand, and early historic North India on the other (Ray 2002: 351).

Gogte (2002), based on the XRD-analysis Rouletted Ware and the associated fine ware from Arikamedu, Alagankulam and other sites on the Coromandel coast, inferred that they were produced in the Bengal region (Chandraketugrah). Citing the similarity of bricks and other materials from Tamil Nadu and Bengal region, he argues that megalithic people might have procured horse and Rouletted Ware from Bengal in exchange of iron weapons. He emphasizes on the external factors as the catalytic agent for the emergence of cities : these 'trade-kings' (from Bengal) must have maintained an army, established ports at several places such as Arikamedu, and Kaveripattinam on the east coast of India between 250 and 200 BC and continued to operate them at least up to 200 AD. Thus they controlled the maritime trade from Bengal to Sri Lanka. They also ruled to sizeable region of south India during the early historic period. Trade in this instance could be described as a state owned' enterprise (Gogte, 2002 : 64).

3.5.3 Genesis and Development of Urbanizm in Tamilakam

The genesis and development of the urbanism in Tamilakam is discussed here through an analysis of some of the important criteria such as demography, territoriality, town planning, architecture, trade and exchange networks.

Growth of Population and Territoriality Divisions

Settlement Pattern : Site Hierarchy, Rural and Urban Settlements

Archaeological research reveals an increase in the number of settlements their size and diversity of material objects in the Early Historic period when compared to he Iron Age. Despite the lack of comprehensive settlement data for the study area, data from a few regional studies support this inference. For example, studies in the Upper Gundar Basin revealed eight Early Historic settlements with Russet-coated painted ware in contract to only one site of the Iron Age remains (Selvakumar 1997). From the analysis of the site size, it is clear the settlements that can be characterized as rural in the Gundar Basin usually cover less than 5 ha and the same is the case in the Upper Palar Basin in Northern Tamil Nadu (Darsana 1997), while the urban centers of Tamilakam range from 7.5 ha to 81 ha (cf. Shanmugam 1997). There is a discrepancy regarding the exact size of the settlements. Different publications mention varying sizes for the same site. According to Shanmugam, Arikamedu measures 33.75 ha, however, systematic site maps prepared by Begley et al. (1996) indicate that the site covers about 7.5 ha. Since the excavations are restricted to limited area and most of the sites are covered by medieval settlements, it is difficult to determine the exact size of Early Historic occupation at several sites. Kaveripattinam has multiple sites covering an area of 10 Sq. km, with a few of them having medieval occupation. Thus, determining the site size during the Early Historic period is not possible. Site hierarchy is reported in the Pennar and Vellar Basins (Rajesh and Arun Raj 2003) and Pudukkottai region (Rajan 2003), where the site area ranges from 2 to 20 ha (Fig.24).

References to various types of settlements such as Kudilur (settlement), sirikudi (small settlement) perur (large settlement) pattanam (port or coastal town) nagar (city), managar and moodur (old city) in the Sangam literature are suggestive of a settlement hierarchy. Cities are mentioned in the literature as rich in wealth ('the righ Muciri', Ahananuru, 149:11) or encircled by fortifications (Devakunjari, 1979; Suresh, 1989) or as the residence of chieftains, while a settlement of the fishing community, the parathavars, is mentioned as sirukudi (small settlement, Ahananuru, 140:1) and that of shell bangle makers as ceris (Maduraikanchi, 136). This emphasizes the settlement hierarchy and disparity in the economic prosperity of the settlements. The descriptions found in the literature reveal that the cities were the foci of a number of activities and those non-local traders were frequently present. From the allusions in the Sangam literature, clear distinction is also noticed in the life-ways of urban and rural settlements (Balasubramanian 1994: 29-33).

The growth in the number of settlements and the site hierarchy in the Early Historic period are clear indicators of population growth and varying population density at these settlements. The demographic increase cannot be attributed to external factors alone. Internal dynamics such as effective application of iron technology and increased variety of crops and rice production in particular were critical to this development. Different types of settlements such as markets and ports, pastoral settlements and, hunter gatherer settlements were present. The urban centers were generally multi-functional, combining resource mobilization production, distribution and administration of resources, maintenance of civic amenities, etc. (e.g. Madurai). The interactions among the Tamil micro zones led to the formation of territorial divisions called nadus, controlled by chieftains from their settlements (mudur), which began to grow as commercial centers subsequently (Selvakumar 2008).

Movement of the people

The Sangam Literature refers to movement of people from one tinai (landscape) to another tinai in order to earn wealth, especially from kurinji (mountainous zone) and mullai (pastoral zone) to marutam (riverine zone) and neytal (coastal zone) where cities began to develop. The poems frequently mention about the hero being away in search of wealth, while the heroine was in deep distress in separation (e.g. Ahananuru, 123). The panas (bards) who were on movement to the courts of the chieftains praising them for gifts are discussed in the Arrupadai. There are also references to people, who went to areas where foreign languages were spoken in search of wealth, and the belief that not travelling for earning will lead to poverty (Ahananuru 127: 17). The Sirupanarrupadi refers to itinerant merchants. These movements and interactions of people seem to have triggered for formation of urban centres at a few places. Migrations of traders from North India, Sri Lanka and neighbouring regions also triggered maritime trade.

Town Planning and Architecture

The majority of urban settlements reveal evidence of brick structure (generally measuring 39-42 × 16-18 × 5-7 cm) and the architectural remains date back to 1st century BC. Remains of burnt bricks and roof tiles (triple grooves with double perforations) are commonly found at the sites datable mainly to the later phase (post-first century BC) of the Early Historic. Kaveripattinam has evidence for the earliest brick construction. The Early Tamil literature does give reference to large mansions, wide streets, markets and fortifications (Maduraikanchi 11, 18-20: 350-356; Pattinapalai 142-145; Ahananuru 124:6; 227). Some of the cities had fortification with moats and ramparts (Suresh 1989 and Devakunjari 1979 : 44-48) and early Madurai was fortified town and there are also references in the literature to moats and ramparts in this city. However, so far archaeological excavations have not revealed no such monumental buildings but for the warehouse at Arikamedu. This is perhaps due to the lack of horizontal excavations. Arimakedu, the only extensively excavated site, has exposed drains, tanks and warehouses, and the orientation of the buildings at this site reveals a planned layout. Remains of a chaitya were found at Kanchipuram (Raman 1987). The material assemblage of certain ceramic forms, bricks, tiles, etc. found at sites such as Arikamedu, Kaveripumpattinam, Korkai and Pattanam shows pan-Indian similarity, and perhaps resulted due to external contacts (Selvakumar 2008).

Crafts and Craft Specialization

Archaeological and textual sources shed light on craft productions and craft specialization in ancient Tamilakam (Rajan, 2001). Among the crafts, iron smelting (Arunraj 2000; Srinivasan and Ranganathan, 2004), pottery making and stone bead making were perhaps well established in the Iron Age itself. Such specialized craftsmen had established settlements all over the region to meet the widespread demand for their products. In the Early Historic period, gem stone cutting, shell and glass bead industries were prominent. Textile industry flourished as revealed by the evidence of spindle-whorls, a piece of woven cloth from Kodumanal, and structures identified as dyeing vat from Uraiyur and Arikamedu, and the reference to various types of cloths in the Sangam and Greco-Roman literature. Perhaps the craftsmen were concentrated in or near the urban centers or near the source of raw material. According to Champakalakshmi (1996) fulltime craft specialization was not established during the Iron Age. Details on nature of the craftsmen and their organization, if any, like their counterparts of the Deccan who had their own guilds (Ray 1985), are not available. However, the reference to craftsmen with specific name and ceris (exclusive colonies) of shell bangle makers mentioned in the Sangam literature points to their prominence and are suggestive of existence of some kind of organization among the craftsmen and perhaps full-time work in the urban areas. Distinct references to goldsmiths and gold merchants indicates that craftsmen and traders were separate communities.

Commodities produced from the crafts were internally consumed, as revealed from the distribution of a variety gold ornaments, glass beads, shell bangles and stone beads, in the settlements of interior Tamil Nadu, and as evidenced by the literary sources (Ahananuru 125: 1). Definitely these commodities were also exported to other regions. Ptolemy's reference to the cloth variety of Argartic is an evidence for the increased demand for such fine products outside Tamil Nadu. Thus the internal consumption and external trade appear to have facilitated fulltime specialization, especially in the post-first century BC scenario (Selvakumar 2008).

Table 2: Crafts and Craft Specialization in Ancient Tamil Country

Crafts	Type of Evidence and reference
Shell working and	Arch: Shell bangle and waster fragments from pearl Fishery archaeological sites (Begley et.al., 1996), Lit: Ref. to shell cutters (Muduraikanchi 511-522), and pearly fishery (Athiyaman 2000).
Stone bead making &	Arch: Glass beads in various stages of manufacturer
Gem cutting	(Kodumanal, Rajan, 1994, 2001). Lit: Ref to people who perforate beads (Maduraikanchi 511-522)
Glass bead making Carpentry/wood working	Arch: bead wasters at Arikamedu (Francis 1987). Arch :Wooden artifacts from Arikamedu (Francis 1987). Ins: Ref to Tacchan, Carpenter (Mahadevan, 2003: 142). Lit : Ref to different types boats & woodworkers.
Crafts	**Type of Evidence and reference**
Pottery making	Arch : Ceramics and terracotta from archaeological sites. Lit : Reg to potters.
Iron working	Arch: Furnace, slag of iron from archaeological sites. Lit : Ref to blacksmiths and their equipment in literature.

contd....

Textile Manufacture	Arch: Brick tank identified as dyeing vat at Uraiyur (Raman, 1988); Spindle-Whorls; woven cotton fabric from Kodumanal (Rajan, 1994, 2001).
Gold working	Arch: Gold ornaments from Megaliths and habitation sites. Ponkolvan (gold trader). In Alagarmalai inscriptions; a touch stone (perumpadankal) in Khuan Luk Pat (Thailand): (Mahadevan, 2003 : 142). Lit : Ref to Goldsmith (Maduraikanchi 511-522).
Bronze working	High-tin bronze artifacts from megaliths and copper coins of the Sangam kings. Silver working Silver rings with Tamil_ Brahmi inscriptions.

Ref: (Selvakumar 2008: 337-370)
Arch: Archaeological, Ins: Inscriptional, Lit : Literary

CHAPTER FOUR

MATERIAL CULTURE

4.1 Ceramic Assemblage – an Introduction

Ceramic traditions and techniques undergo changes because of a number of factors that include modifications in the social, economic and cultural components of a society, and external influence- contacts, and movement of people, ideas and goods. In the Early Historic Tamilakam during the course of urbanization numerous changes occurred in the ceramic traditions. This Chapter discusses the characteristics of the ceramic of the Iron Age and early historic periods in Tamil Nadu and Kerala.

There is a lack of clarity in the use of terms such as 'megalithic', 'iron age', and 'early historic' in some of the texts on the archaeology of south India. Here, 'iron age' is defined as the period spanning between 1000 BC and 300 BC, and 'early historic', between 300 BC and the 500 AD. Megalithism is viewed as a burial tradition that appeared in the Iron Age and continued in the early historic. The Iron Age was characterized by the presence of plain and white varieties of Black and Red Ware (BRW), megalithic burials and iron objects (Gururaja Rao, 1972; Leshnik 1974; Moorti 1994). The early historic period saw the introduction of Russet Coated Painted ware (RCP), fine Rouletted Ware and imported ceramics such as amphora and terra sigillata (Arretine), while certain ceramics and material culture of the Iron Age continued. However, it is not always possible to distinguish the Iron Age megaliths fom the early historic megaliths, except in the cases where Russet Coated and Painted Ware or there chronological markers are found or C14 dates are available. Hence, the terms megalithic and megalith are used sometimes to denote the burials of Iron Age and early historic periods together (Selvakumar 2008).

4.1.1 Black-and-Red Ware

Black and Red ware with black interior and red-exterior - occurs in India from the Chalcolithic period onwards in various cultural contexts (Singh 1982). It is typical of megalithic or Iron Age of South India and it continuous in to early historic period. The pottery was fired between 500° C and 600°C (Gurumurthy 1981: 268) using inverted firing technique, and the lustrous polish on the surface is attributed to the debatable 'salt glazing' (Wheeler 1948). The common vessel forms in this ware, which primarily served as tableware, include dishes and bowls with simple rim and with sager base (Soundrarajan 1994: 47), and jars. This pottery was thin bodied/sectioned in the Iron Age and becomes thicker in the early historic period (Maski, Period III: Thapar 1957 : 76; Perur: Gurumurthy 1981 : 156). Though predominant during the Iron Age, this pottery began to decline in popularity in the early historic period (e.g. Uraiyur: Raman 1988: 13), and is absent or rarely present in several early historic assemblages/contexts, e.g. Northern Sector at Rikamedu, Kanchipuram, Vasuvasamudram and Kaveripattinak (Soudararajan 1994: 42, footnote). However, it continued to be used in burial context. This pottery was widely used till about 500 AD (e.g. Thirukampuliyur : Raman 1988: 31), and perhaps survived in the early medieval period, in a very limited frequency (Raman 1988: 13). The upper limit of this ceramics is not known. But definitely, BRW must have come into use in the beginning of the first millennium BC in Tamil Nadu.

However, more C14 dates are needed to ascertain the early presence of this pottery in this region.

During the present survey this pottery (B&R) was discovered from many sites like Parikal (Fig. 25 and Pl. 43), Sengamedu, Tiruvakkarai, Suttukeni and Karaimedu. Since the region around Arikamedu abounds in Megalithic sites its presence suggests that they had some sort of commercial and cultural links with Arikamedu.

4.1.2 Coarse Grey Ware

This Ware is a medium to coarse pottery with surface colour approaching white. Coarse Gray Ware is a distinct pottery that is so far reported only from Arikamedu in Pre-Arretine and Arretine levels in the Northern Sector without the association of BRW (Wheeler et. Al., 1946; Begley et al., 1996). This ware, which decreases in frequency in the Post-Arretine levels, has quite distinct forms from BRW of Iron Age and early historic period. The Coarse Grey Ware has been confused with the Neolithic pottery (Sundara 1987). However, it is a wheel-made pottery, quite distinct from Neolithic ware (which was handmade), though some similarity is noticed in vessel forms (Selvakumar 2008).

During the present survey this (grey ware) pottery has been collected from the surface of the Tirasu (near Vallupuram).

4.1.3 Coarse Red Ware

This ware (CRW) is found both in the megalithic burials and habitation contexts of site in both Iron Age and Early Historic periods. This pottery has a slip or wash, and it did not require any additional treatments. Sometimes, it is also referred to as Red Slipped Ware, Orange Slipped Ware with a medium fabric. CRW is generally in low proportion in the Iron Age, but more commonly encountered in the Early Historic and later sites (e.g. Uraiyur : Raman, 1988: 53). This type of pottery, which does not require any special treatment, became popular from the early historic period onwards. Cooking vessels, jars, large storage jars and urns are the common forms of CRW, which sometimes has a red slip. While the BRW decreases in frequency in the early historic, the CRW increases. At Arikamedu CRW increased in popularity, whereas the coarse grey ware declined in Southern Sector, which represents the later occupation. In the production of thin-bodied vessels, clay was sieved to removed the large stone particles and in the case of large jars straw and husk were added as tempering materials.

This ware was reported during the present survey from Tirasu, Thirusopuram, Manikolai and Parikal (Fig. 26-27 and Pl.44). In both the places this ware is unearthed along with glass beads.

4.1.4 Fine Wares (Rouletted, Grey and other Wares)

An assemblage of very fine pottery appears in the early historic context at Arikamedu, Nattamedu (Karaikadu), Kaveripattinam, Alagamkulam and several other sites in Tamil Nadu and sites in South India (Fig. 28). They include Rouletted Ware dish (Arikamedu, Wheeler et. Al. 1946, Types 1 and 2), stamped bowl (Arikamedu, Wheeler et al. 1946, Type 10), bowl with ring foot (Arikamedu, Wheeler et al. 1946, Type 18), plate with stamped decorations (Arikamedu, Wheeler et al. 1946, Type 129) and Fine Grey Ware (Arikamedu, Wheeler et al. 1946, Type 44), very distinct from the Coarse Grey Ware mentioned above, (Arikamedu, Wheeler et al. 1946, Types 6 and 44). A few of these fine wares, especially Rouletted Ware, are reported from Berenike (Tomber 2000), Sri Lanka (Deraniyagala 1992) and Indonesia (Walker and Santoso 1977; Ardika and Bellwood, 1991; Ardika et al., 1993; Gogte 1997, 2002) (Fig. 10).

Among these fine wares, Rouletted Ware is widely distributed in India and is present at numerous sites in Tamil Nadu (Fig. 11). Other fine wares are mainly found at Arikamedu, Nattamedu (Kudikadu) and Alagankulam in the coastal region of Tamil Nadu in a large quantity, may be around 10% of the total ceramics, whereas at inland settlements such as Uraiyur, Karur and Kanchipuram in Tamil Nadu. It is distributed even at remote settlements of Tamil Nadu such as T. Kallupatti and S.

Pappinayakkanpatti in Madurai District. The Rouletted Ware has black, black-and-red, and red ware varieties. Arikamedu mostly has black, grey and black-and-red varieties.

The rim and body sherds of Rouletted Ware which do not show rouletting decoration are generally treated as a distinct ware. Gurumurthy (1981: 146, pl. 16a) reports a grey ware sherd at Kanchipuram with inscription and it appears to be the rim sherd of Rouletted Ware of fine ware. The Vanagiri inlet-sluice site at Kaveripattinam has buff-grey fine ware (Soundararajan 1994: 50) which appears to belong to this group. This pottery at Chandraketgarh is described as Black and Red Ware (Chakraborthy 2000). This Balck and Red ware is distinct from the megalithic Black and Red Ware, which has a coarser fabric.

Based on scientific analysis a single source is attributed to the Rouletted ware and the related fine ware ceramics (Ardika et al. , 1993; Krishnan and Conningham 1995; Gogte 1997; Ford et al. n.d.). Earlier it was though that this ceramics was produced in the Mediterranean region. On the basis of XRD – analysis, Gogte proposed that this pottery was perhaps produced in to Chandraketugarh-Tamluk region of West Bengal (Gogte 1997 & 2002). However, the two sherds from Satanikota indicate that they were produced locally (Ghosh, 1986: 151). The analysis made by Selvakumar on coarse ware pottery from Arikamedu, and the observation on cereamics from the Chandraketugarh in the collection of Dr. Sharmi Chakraborthy point out the possibility of Rouletted Ware source being in Bengal region. However, more samples of clay and from different regions of South India need to be analysed to test the hypothesis proposed by Gogte (1997).

An imitated version of Rouletted Ware of coarse ware fabric is found at several sites including Arkamedu (Wheeler et. Al., 1946), Kanchipuram (Gurumurthy 1981: 146), Vasavasamumdram (Gurumurthy 1981: 147) and Perur (Gurumurthy 1981: 157). Black and Red Ware at Kilayur wharf site have imitated Rouletted Ware designs (Selvakumar 2008).

During the present survey Rouletted sherds were discovered from three sites viz. Tirasu, Kottaimedu and Karaimedu (Pl.45 and 46). Maligaimedu, which is adjoining Tirasu many Early Historical artifacts have been reported including Rouletted shreds. At Tirasu, Rouletted sherds have been discovered. Whereas at other two sites, (i.e. Kottaimedu & Karaimedu) very few sherds of Rouletted variety were unearthed. Totally fifteen body sherds and a rim of Rouletted ware found on the surface of the above mentioned sites. None have fine fabric, although the collected sherds are studied and compared with Arikamedu. A rim fragment of Rouletted Ware has a similar form with the Wheeler Type 3b (see Wheeler et al. 1946: 53, Fig. 8). It is a highly damaged, weathered rim sherd, with no traces of slip. In core, it is black, well grained coarse ware without any inclusions, and the texture is compact. All the body sherds have the same fabric except one sherd. All the body sherds surfaces are weathered, although the slip is visible on both sides. Only one convex-side body sherd has fine surface with traces of red slip on the exterior and black on the interior. The fabric is red, grained coarse with a well closed texture. Very few of the body sherds have the Rouletting decorations.

4.1.4.1 Red Polished Ware

Red Polished ware is a rare ceramic category so far reported from Arikamedu (Begley 1996 b: 129, Fig. 4, 9, 13), Pallavaneeshwaram and Kareripattinam (Sundararajan 1994 : 72, Fig. 17.1, bottle-necked Kushan sprinkler) in Tamil Nadu. This pottery is mainly concentrated in Gujarat region (Orton 1991). At Satanikota, Rouletted Ware and RCP ware were introduced earlier than Red Polished ware, and is found in limited quantity (0.2% Ghosh 1986: 102). It appears at Hastinapur and at a few sites in the Ganga valley (Lal 1954-55, period iv, Pl. 10, xv, a-b). Red polished ware is also found at Anuradhapura in Sri Lanka (Deraniyagala 1992). What is reported as 'Red Polished ware' at Vasvasamudram (Gurumurthy 1981: 147) does not seem to be the true

Red Polished Ware, but only a coarse red ware with polished surfaces. Red Ware sprinklers found from Kanchipuram near he Stupa remains (Gurumurthy 1981: 142, Note 91) is not similar to the original Red Polished Ware. During the present survey this ware was collected only from Manikolai as surface find (Pl.47).

4.1.4.2 Amphora

Amphora is a large conical double-handled Mediterranean wine-jar. Buff in colour and made of well-levitated clay. In India, such jars occur both in the stratified contexts as well as isolated finds. The distribution pattern of the amphora presents a contrasting picture to that of the Rouletted Ware. While most of the Rouletted Ware sites are on the east coast, the amphora sites are heavily concentrated on the west, along the coast of Maharashtra and Gujarat. On the basis of the associated finds (including coins) and stratigraphic context (in the case of excavated sites), the import of the amphora in India has been assigned to the 1st century AD. But recent studies indicate that amphora did begin to reach Arikamedu as early as 1st century BC, if not even slightly earlier. At least two sherds from the site have been identified as fragments of Graeco-Italic jars of the 2nd century BC (Pl. 48 and 49). In addition, Arikamedu, this ware has been reported from several sites in Tamil Nadu Alagankulam, Karur (Nagaswamy 1995), Vasuvasamudram (Nagaswamy and Abdul Majeed 1978) and Pattanam in Kerala (Tomber 2005).

Unlike the Rouletted Ware, the amphora was a costly item. Only a few kingdoms that enjoyed political stability and economic prosperity, such as Satavahana, Kshatrapa, Kushan and early Tamil kingdoms, could afford to purchase the Roman wine; all the known amphorae, belong to these regions. It is of considerable significance to note that amphorae have been reported only from the urban centers of the Early Historic Tamilakam (Suresh 1992; 47). These were centers of commercial, religious and political importance with sizeable elite population engaged in cultivating exotic habits. Even in the Tamil Sangam works, there is a clear indication that Roman wine, known for its high quality and fragrance, was meant mainly for the kings and nobles alone (the ruling elite) (Purananura 56, 17-21).

Until recently, it was generally accepted that the amphora was mainly used to store the Mediterranean wine which was in great demand throughout India. Chemical analysis of some sherds revealed traces of a resinous substance on the interior of the jar. This was either a resin applied to the interior to reduce its porosity or it resulted from wine as a residue sticking to the inner walls of amphora. The results from the archaeo-chemical studies have been amply corroborated by the early Tamil literature which makes copious references to the import of wine in India. The Periplus also categorically states that wine was one of the chief items of import into Indian ports. But very recent studies on the amphorae finds in India have, however, definitely indicated that the amphora was used to contain, besides wine, a variety of other substances such as foodstuffs (including garum, a Spanish fish sauce), olive oil and medicines. In Arikamedu alone, for example, there are several fragments of olive-oil jars from the northern Adriatic area and a few (at least nine) sherds of Campanian wine jars of the 1st century BC anc 1st century AD. Therefore, the presence of amphorae does not necessarily indicate trade in wine. The amphorae in the Buddhist sites of northern and western India may indicate a demand in the Buddhist establishments for items like olive oil (which was certainly an item of Roman export to India) rather than wine. Again, the finds of garum jars in Arikamedu clearly suggests that there was a Roman settlement at the site since garum was a prized item in the diet of the early Romans and the sauce was certainly not of interest to the Indians. In any case, there is no evidence to show that garum was an item of trade between the Romans and the Indians. Foodstuffs may have been brought by the maritime Romans along with them for their own consumption.

During the present survey a body fragment of an amphora has been discovered from Kottaimedu. The size of the sherd is measured to 5cm x 6cm and the thickness is 1.2cm, the wheel marks are visible on the interior red surface. The exterior is reddish yellow with black inclusions on the medium surface. The paste is hard and compact throught red in colour with black and white inclusions of 1 mm. size. It is identified as a knidian amphora fragment; possibly from Greek island Knidos. The traders may have brought Knidan wine to India. This type is generally dated 1st century BC.

Amphorae similar to Knidian are found at more sites in India, but for the moment, Knidian fragment presence at Kottaimedu coupled with strong appearance in Egypt suggest that they have reached Kottaimedu, through Arikamedu, by the Red-sea routes.

4.1.4.3 Arretine Ware (Terra Sigillata)

Terra Sigillata (Arretine) is Mediterranean tableware, known only from Arikamedu so far in India (Slane 1996). Though there are claims of it's discover from several sites, its identity is yet to be confirmed.

4.1.4.4 Conical Jar

Conical jars erroneously terms as 'amphorae' or 'imitation amphorae' have been reported from Arikamedu (Wheeler et al., 1946, Types 74 and 75), Nattamedu (Kudikudu), Vasuvasumudram (Nagasamy and Abdul Majeed 1978) (Pl.50) and Kanchipuram (Begley 1996b:233-234). At Kanchipuram such jars are found planted in a row on the ground level (Raman 1991). This type is restricted to northern part of Tamil Nadu and recently a few toe sherds of this jar have been found at Pattanam in Kerala (Shajan et al., 2004). This form appears to have been inspired by the amphora jar, though what can be considered cas prototype is found in the megalithic fabric at Arikamedu (Casal 1949: Fig. 9).

Unlike the genuine amphorae, these handle-less jars are of very coarse fabric and are mostly dull red in colour, though the specimens from Arikamedu were reported to be grey or grayish-red (Fig. 12 and 29). The conical jars usully have a height of about 1 m, and the thickness of the walls (of the jars) range from 2 to 3 cm and diameter of the conical bottom is 3 to 6 cm. At Kanchi, the jars were found buried in straight rows – probably the remnants of a wine cellar or a small bar. Smaller jars placed within bigger onces were noticed at Arikamedu and Kanchi but not at Vasavasamudram. As the conical jars, due to their very shape, had to be placed underground, small jars could have been fitted inside the larger ones to enhance the strength and thickness of the container. The conical jars have no slip, generally but a few examples at Arikamedu had a slip which was invariably confined to the portion above the shoulder. Another interesting feature is that, at Arikamedu, some of the jars where completely wheel-turned while othcrs were hand-made up to a certain height from the base, above which they were wheel-turned. At Arikamedu, the conical jars occur in strata of the 1st century AD or even slightly earlier along with the original amphora, whereas at other sites the conical jars were in vogue at a later date. It could thus be concluded that the earliest conical jars were produced and used at Arikamedu, which was a major pottery-manufacturing center and from here the jar, and the technique of its manufacture spread to other sites in Tamil Nadu.

During the present survey 2 bottom pieces of conical jar were discovered along the sea shore of Thirusopuram (Pl.51), which is located about 15 km east of Cuddalore town. These pieces basically Coarse Red Ware in nature because ill fired which can be seen from the section of the jars. Both the conical jars are about 7cm in length. The associated findings of conical jars like Black and Red Ware, Coarse Red Ware and a good number of glass beads indicate this place had some sort of contact with or acted as satellite settlement of Arikamedu.

4.1.4.5 Stamped Bowl/Cup

Bowls with flat base, diagonal sides (inverted trapezoidal in section) with stamped impressions of fish, peacock and bird motifs between multiple grooves in fine ware occur at the coastal sites of Arikamedu (Wheeler et al., 1946: Type 10), Nattamedu and Alagankulam. It has been encountered at Berenike in Egypt (Tomer, 2000: Pl.12). The fabric of this ware is similar to Rouletted Ware, and it is not reported from Iron Age 'megalithic' context.

Bowls similar to the above but without stamp (flat base and slanting sides) are found at Arikamedu (Wheeler et al., 1946: Type 12, 12a) and present at Taxila (Ghosh, 1948: Types 4-5, Fig.4). A variant is seen a Taxila but with a disc base (Ghosh, 1948: 15c of Pl. 7). Though no stamped bowl/cup was discovered during he present survey, a fragment of ribbed glass bowl has been discovered on the surface of Kottaimedu in Pondicherry region. Interestingly in the excavations of Arikamedu this type of glass bowl fragments were found and some of them were published. The fragment of a transparent blue glass bowl with horizontal ridges is dated to Sheeler's pre-Arretine levels. It might have come from Arikamedu and perhaps traveled from one of the Red-sea ports along the same route as the Knidian amphora on its way to Kottaimedu.

4.1.5 Graffiti and Inscriptions

Post-firing graffiti marks very commonly occur on the megalithic burial and habitation pottery and their significance is as yet not clear. They are considered as marks of clans or family (Rajan and Bopearachchi, 2002). Different burials have distinct graffiti marks. The megalithic graffiti are mainly symbolic and pictorial graffiti were nearly absent in the Iron Age. During the present survey potsherds with graffiti symbol have been discovered from Parikal (Pl.52) and Tirasu (both are located near Villapuram town). While Parikal graffiti is available on Black &

red ware and Red Polished ware, in Tirasu graffiti symbols are only on B&R ware.

Pictorial Graffiti

There is an increase in the pictorial graffiti in the Early Historic period. At Arikamedu, human figures are found on pottery (Wheeler et al., 1946 : Plate XL). A graffito of ship is found at Alagankulam (Casson, 1997; Begley n.d.). Though the exact purpose of such sketches is not known, perhaps, they were used as models or for practice by the artists, who executed these images on different media (Selvakumar 2008).

Inscriptions

Short inscriptions in Tamil-Brahmi and Prakrit mentioning individual names are found on pottery from several sites in Early Historic context in Tamil Nadu (Mahadevan, 2004). Many of the inscriptions are fragmentary and the complete ones read 'Muthukuluran Akal' (the dish of Muthukuluran), 'Varuniya Akal' (the dish of Varuni) (Koodumanal) indicating ownership of the vessels. Sometimes they give the place name of the individual (Wheeler et al. 1946; Rajan 1994).

Functions

Ceramics were used for various purposes such as ritualistic, storage and transportation and cooking.

Ritualistic

Burial urn with pointed base was a common receptacle used for placing the mortal remains of the dead in the Iron Age – Early Historic period. Sometimes large vessels were used as lid for covering the urns instead of capstones. Sarcophagi were used in certain contexts for burials. These forms did not seem to have changed in the early historic period. The tub-like pottery and pottery with Brahmi letter "Ma' symbol might have been used for ritual purposes.

Storage and Transportation

Large storage jars resembling megalithic urns in shape are found frequently in the Early Historic period. The Early Historic specimens are well fired and sturdier.

The conical jars of Arikamedu (Wheeler et al., 1946 Types 764-75) and Kanchipuram were new types developed for storage and transportation of liquids. Probably, they were an imitation of Roman wine amphorae.

Cooking

Another innovation of the Early Historic period has been the portable oven (Arikamedu Wheeler et al., 1946: Type 148). It is not reported from Iron Age contexts. Therefore, it seems to be an innovation in the early historic period. Besides, more varieties of cooking vessels and frying pans, especially wide-mouthed, in contrast to the narrow mouthed vessels of the iron age, appear in the Early Historic context (e.g. Arikamedu: Wheeler et al., 1946: Types 24 and 95).

Table Ware

Fine, deluxe table wares appear in the Early Historic period mainly due to trade activities. Rouletted ware dishes (Arimakedu:Wheeler et al., 1946) – Types 1 and 2, fine Grey Ware of Type 6 – were used for serving food. At Arikamedu a trench in Southern Sector had chiken bones on a broken Rouletted Ware dish, which appeared to be leftover of a meal (Begley et al., 2004). Perhaps it served as a sort of 'Chinse Wares' of the Early Historic period. Terra Sigillata was a table ware. The imported terra sigillata and Roman glassware could have been used by certain restricted groups (Selvakumar 2008).

Industrial Purposes

Ceramics were used for industrial purposes in the early historic period. Traces of industrial activities are noticed at several sites in the early historic of Tamil Nadu context. At Arikamedu pottery with glass slag remains were found from surface context. Terracotta spindles used in weaving industry are found at several sites in Tamil Nadu (Rajan 1994).

4.2 Antiquities

4.2.1 Terracotta Figurines

Terracotta comprise of human and animal forms and other objects of utilitarian nature, such as toys and playthings including objects of ornamental value. Many pieces made in stucco have also been reported, which comprise of mouldings, lathe-turned devices including some with intricate patterns. As a matter of fact, more varieties have been found among utilitarian objects of day-today use in terracotta. Some ear-ornaments have been found bearing designs, indentations in geometric patterns and flower decorations of high artistic quality. Bangles, pendants, hair pins and rings are also reported of which some have been found with designs carved on them. All these indicate the artistic decorations on terracotta have an earlier origin and sustained continuously later mainly for the reason that they were affordable and could be made in large quantity by the use of the mould. Even though terracotta tradition was not deep rooted and had an early beginning in the Deccan and further north, the decorative devices adopted in the burial ceramics of the Iron Age times with animal headed knobs, flower motifs and other patterns have relevance in our understanding of the continuity in subsequent times. The clear cut interaction and technological traditions adopted and the cultural outcome are of very great interest. A detailed study of the various aspects of terracotta art is yet to be attempted.

Sites that have yielded terracotta include Alagarai, Arikamedu, Appukallu, Adiyamankottai, Boluvampatti, Kanchipuram, Kaveripattinam, Korkai, Tirukkampuliyur, Uraiyur, etc. The objects consist of human-male and female figurines, toys and play things such as discs, hopscotch, games man, ornamental objects such as finger rings, beads, bangles, ear-discs etc. At Kaveripattinam, the early terracotta figurines were made from moulds and latter completed by hand finish. Some have early Buddhist affiliations influenced by the developments in Amaravati-Nagarjunakonda. So far no distinctive type could be separated as an independent cultural entity exclusive to this period or area. However, there is an attempt to render the figures realistic which is common at other contemporary places in the Deccan for e.g. half-closed eyes, chubby faces, fleshy cheeks and natural and soft rendering of the body. The early figures are found from about the 1st century AD. At other sites, such as Tirukkampuliyur, Alagarai and Uraiyur though not many figures have been found from early levels, they appear to have a common source of origin. They have been prepared from moulds and then finished by hand and parts of body were affixed at leather hard stage, such a incisions made for ornamentation and other details.

Arikamedu was revealed a female figurine wearing a sari and another figurine with different dress. They appear to be made of wooden moulds. A seal impression of a male figure riding a chariot is found at Arikamedu (Sidebotham, 1996). The terracotta figurines found at Uraiyur appears to be handmade (Raman 1988: 84-92).

During the present field survey humpty numbers of terracotta figurines have been discovered from the study area. Totally twelve figurines have been recovered from Kottapakkatuveli, Thirunavalur, Tirasu and Kattuselur (Pl. 53-55). Almost all of them are human figurines and all were broken. In some of them only the bust portion is available whereas in the remaining figurines leg portion can only be seen. Besides artistic features, the associated materials like Rouletted sherds, brick bats, terracotta rings and structures attest to their early historical age.

4.2.2 Terracotta Lamps

Terracotta lamps from another major feature of the surface collections. Arikamedu has yielded at least three fragments of the Roman lamp, each in different circumstances. During the course of the present field study, lamps were found from Arasur, Sendiampakkam and Siruvalai (Pl. 56 and 57). In general, lamps seem to have been made for everyday use.

4.2.3 Other Terracotta Artifacts

A Spindle whorl, used in spinning thread, discs of terracotta and pottery (Pl. 58 and 59), and ear ornaments are other type of ceramic artifacts (Pl. 60), discovered during exploration and are form Early Historic sites in Tamil Nadu.

4.2.4 Beads

During Early Historical period bead making was a thriving industry. Beads are predominant over other objects. Though no remains of lapidary have been traced, there is sufficient data which bear testimony to the existence of bead making centers, on the basis of density of debit age resulting from bead making process.

At some sites glass beads appear quite early (c.3rd century BC) whereas at others a little later (c. 1st century BC) and in some places much later (c.2nd century AD and after). It develops into a major industry from Early medieval to late times beginning from tenth century onwards. In other words, the data emphasize continuity of glass industry from early times.

Glass bangles and beads have been found both in quantity and variety at Kaveripattinam and nearby places datable from about the 1st century BC. The colour range of glass is green, blue, black and yellow and occur in the shapes of barrel, cylinder-circular, spherical and bicone-hexagonal. Glass bangle is next in popularity in colour of blue, green, yellow and red. Not many occur at lower levels, but increase in later levels (c. 4th century AD and after). Evidence suggests possibly a local industry.

Equally rich are the finds semi-precious stones, paste, copper and terracotta at several areas of Kaveripattinam such as Kilaiyur, Manigramam, Vanagiri and Pallavaeshwaram occurring from the 2nd century BC to the 3rd- 4th century AD, made from popular shapes are barrel, spherical, cylinder, circular and hexagonal. Some belong to collared variety. Such a large quantity of their presence at the site of Kaveripattinam suggests a local industry. Equally significant is the occurrence of a large number of beads at Kanchipuram made of semi-precious stones, paste, glass and terracotta occurring in levels of the third-second century BC. Its continued occurrence in large number in late levels is noteworthy. There were multiple centers of bead production.

At alagarai and Thirukampuliyur a variety of beads have been found made from semi-precious stones, paste and steatite from the early levels of occupation; soapstone is the popular material at Tirukkampuliyur, agate, chalcedony, Jasper, amethyst and rock crystal beads are common. They are made in shapes such as spherical, rectangular, barrel and also with faceted surface. At both places, tiny disc beads made of in semi-precious stones, particularly of which soap stone is more popular. The shapes are barrel, circular, square and elliptical. Some are collared ones. Beads occur from early levels onwards.

A variety of beads have also been reported from Alagankulam. They are made from early times made from semi-precious stones, steatite and paste. Carnelian is most preferred raw material. Pendants have also been prepared from carnelian. Similarly beads are present at Korkai and Vasuvasamudram as well as at sites identified with burials, habitation. Appukallu, Adiyamankottai, Perur and T. Kallupatti hoards of beads occur at Early Historic levels.

Situated close to the coastal region near Cuddalore, at Karaikadu evidence of a lapidary has been found. A brick structure, and bead making supported by evidence of beads in varying stages of manufacture, including a scatter of raw material cores and lumps – all of which are ascribable to c. 1st century AD have been unearthed at Karaikadu. Such details are known for the first time.

By far the richest evidence is known from Arikamedu ever since excavations carried out by Wheeler in 1944-45. A study of the baeds has revealed that the bead industry was a dominant industrial activity at the town in the heyday of its existence as an international harbour. It was a manufacturing and marketing center for beads and bangles made of semi-precious stones and glass. Arikamedu was a bead maritime emporium where every sort of baed made from anywhere in the world could be bought and sold. A systematic documentation of the glass objects carried out at Arikamedu has revealed that it was not only a major workshop center for manufacture of glass objects, but also varieties of them have been traded on a large scale.

Source of Glass

Mediterranean glass antiquities have been discovered in a few sites in the north-west, west and south. The finds mostly belong to the period between 1st centry BC and 1st century AD.

The Periplus contains copious references to the import of glass to India. The reference to 'several sorts of coloured glasses' in the Periplus (6, 7, 17) may include glass beads of various colours. References to glass in early Indian literature are, however, meager. In Tamil Sangam Literature there is no reference to 'glass objects', 'glass production' or 'glass-trade' despite its presence in various sites in Tamil Nadu. Whereas a few glass beads from the Arikamedu collection have been identified as imports from the Rome (Sures 2004: 137). Some of these are reported to be imitation of onyx beads which were manufactured at Arikamedu and sold to Rome. Glass beads from none of the other sites in India are believed to be authentic imports from the Mediterranean region. It should however, be noted that the beads finds from many of the Indian sites, especially those in the extreme south, have not been thoroughly investigated. It is plausible that some may have been imported from the west. Glass beads imported from Rome have been recently found in the stratified contexts at Mantai (Sri Lanka). In any case, the import of glass raw material or glass beads into India was on a small scale (Sures : 2004; 137).

During the present survey two Early Historical sites viz. Manikolai and Thirusopuram (both in modern Cuddalore district of Tamil Nadu) have been identified where dense scatter of glass beads have been identified (see Pl. 34 and 38). These glass beads are of different colour green, blue, black and yellow and are of the shapes of barrel, cylinder-circular, spherical and bicone-hexagonal. Besides finished beads, both the sites have yielded unfinished beads and wastages (rough outs). These discoveries of beads and their byproducts reconfirm that possible presence of multiple centers of bead manufacture.

4.2.5 Shell Objects

Shell objects constitute the largest among objects of adornment found from many Early Historic sites in Tamil Nadu. It is also one of the oldest industries and the very fact that many different types of shell objects found with variety of decorations in burial sites of the Iron Age indicate their early origins.

Ornamental objects prepared from shell include beads, bangles, pendants, ear-discs, circular head ornaments. Other utilitarian objects include as ladles, spoons, palettes and so on. Shell has a known religious value and is an object of sacred veneration since ancient times. Chank-shell cutting is a local industry in many sites identified with the whole range of repertoire such as chank bits, cut pieces of columela the plain shankha ready for cutting.

Major evidence of shell industry has been found at Tirukkampuliyur. Objects consist of beads, bangles and pieces of cut-shell "showing the stages in the technique of making shell bangles and objects". Many of them found in the trench at Tirukkampuliyur-7 are considered the oldest. The beads are spherical or barrel shaped; bangles are of two types: plain and decorated; the latter done with a sharp instrument and designs consist of straight lines or criss-cross patterns. Some have channel-shaped cross sections possibly for inserting gold foils or other mental fillings for decoration. At Alagarai the largest collection consists of shell beads and bangles belonging to periods I and II (c. 2nd century BC - 6th century AD). Bangles show a variety of designs work mostly geometric patterns. The shapes reveal some common forms such as Plano-convex and concave rectangular. Most of the objects have been known from early levels. Some have been painted in red ochre wash with designs and geometric patterns. In period I at Uraiyur the shell beads are most dominant, they are associated with RCPW and Black and Red Ware, further suggesting an early origin of shell ornaments (c. 3rd century BC). Some bear decorations; one consists of incised vertical grooves and other is a floral design. Bangles have thick and thin square section, unlike those from Alagarai and Thirukkampuliyur. Korkai has also yielded objects of shell amounting to a major local industry. Shell bangle pieces and sawed conches have been found in large numbers. They occur in association with potsherds bearing graffiti. The conches are sawed in between the top and bottom bortion in order to make bangles. No less significant is the finds at Alagankulam of shell objects in good number; conches for bangle manufacture have been found in various stages of making and indicate an extensive conch-shell industry. It is also represented at Arikamedu (Pl.61) though many of them found unfinished stages of preparation. A large number of them found are crescent, ear-ornaments. Shell objects have been reported from many sites mixed with burial and habitation contexts taking back the existence of the industry, a few centuries earlier; for e.g. Appukallu

(District North Arcot) and T. Kallupatti (District Madurai). Other historical sites from where shell objects have been reported include Adiyamankottai (District Dharmpuri), Perur (District Coimbatore), Kambarmedu (District Thanjavur) and Kanchipuram.

Extensive shell cutting has also been identified at Karaikadu where remains of unfinished shell beads and bangles and cut shell pieces have been found in clusters. During the present survey though there is no shell objects found in any of the sites, core of shell (columella) was found at Ulakkur near Villupuram (Pl.62).

CHAPTER FIVE

EARLY HISTORIC TRADE

5.1 Concepts, Theories and Models

Trade and other forms of exchange among people are important aspects of research in the archaeology of early civilization. There has been considerable progress in this area of research resulting in a specialized study of trade and exchange. This area of research has witnessed methodological changes in our approach to understanding the dynamics of trade and exchange.

This chapter discusses the nature of trade during the Early Historic period in the study area: establishing the trade network of the region; listing the commodities, identify their provenance, and trace the river and land routes long which the movement of goods took place. A brief summary of different approaches and models on trade is given below, which is followed by the presentation of literary, inscriptional and archaeological data relating to the study area.

The term trade is difficult to define and requires a comprehensive approach as it covers a wide range of aspects touching on different spheres of human activity. Trade may be defined, in a broad sense, as the exchange of goods through peaceful means (Chang 1975: 211, 221-222: Renfrew 1969:152). It is difficult to differentiate between trade and exchange, if the exchange activity of a particular region is not corroborated by concrete evidence, as exchange is the spatial distribution of materials from hand to hand and social group to social group (Earle 1982: 2), whereas trade involves use of money as well. Adam (1974: 239-245) observes that "ancient trade is often too narrowly identified with habitual patterns in the movement of goods, and the study of trade factor not only requires new field and laboratory data, but also the awareness of ethno-historic, historic and ethnographic studies that are already responsive to a richer and more valid research paradigm". In the study of trade, importance is given to ecology-based geographical units of analysis of progressively increasing size and complexity, with different forms and degrees of social interaction characterizing each. In the study of trade and exchange, a distinction is made between internal exchanges taking place within the specific society, and external trade or exchange where goods are traded over much greater distances, moving from one social unit to another (Renfrew and Bahn 1991).

Two different approaches are being followed by archaeologists in the interpretation of trade: (a) analytical approach which involves typological studies for establishing trade relation between two areas, and (b) theoretical development of models for the identification of the mechanism, institutional framework and social context within which trade operated. These two approaches have their own set of parameters for the study of trade and exchange network.

Analytical Approach

The objective of this approach is to identify the sources of various raw materials and their production centers. There are several scientific methods such as X-Ray Diffraction, X-Ray Fluorscence, Neutron Activation Analysis. Thin Section microscopy, Optical spectroscopy, Beta-ray back-scatter, Petrological analysis and so on, which are helpful in tracing the provenance of ceramics, lithic tools, metals, glass, semi-precious stones, etc. (Renfrew and Bahn 1991: 314-20).

Theoretical Approach

This approach to trade and exchange is largely based on anthropological, geographical and sociological data. This approach plays a crucial role in the comparative studies. The following are the different methods propounded in the studies related to trade mechanism.

I. Substantive Approach

This approach focuses on three aspects namely, supply, demand and market, to reconstruct the network of primitive and ancient societies, since economic activities in these societies are governed by social relationships (Polanya et al. 1957; Dalton 1969). Among reciprocity, redistribution and market, the last one is given more emphasis. The co-relation of exchange systems with social types has been used extensively in archaeology in an evolutionary scheme (Renfrew 1972; Hodder 1978). According to Hodder (1982:200) "Substantist economy is connected with two different types of analyses, the former of output and performance, and the latter of social context of exchange.

II. Formalist Approach

Locational analysis is the prime concern in this approach where distribution of a particular material is taken into consideration for identifying modes of exchange (Renfrew 1969: 157, 1977: 73; Hodder 1982:201). This method helps in judging the amount of an exchanged item found at a site, which is described mathematically as a function of distance of the size of the interaction/transaction centers (Hodder 1982 : 201).

III. Social Exchange Approach

In this approach social transactions constitute the main focus where all sorts of interactions affect family structure and the social patterns (Belshaw 1968 : 95). This approach has been utilized in archaeology by highlighting common access to items of external trade, which can be used as markers of social status and the role of exchange as 'social storage' (Frankenstein and Rowlands 1978; Halstead 1981). It involves the economic concepts of maximization and operation, the dimension of social strategies and the availability of subsistence resources and control over production (Hodder 1982:205).

IV. Symbolic and Ideological Approach

This approach consdrs exchange as more than 'economic', since it takes place within a cultural, ideological and historical context (Hodder 1982: 207-209). It attempts to analyze as to how the symbolism associated with exchanged commodities provides the basis of power for some groups and also the process of legitimization of such power.

V. Trade and System Theory

In this framework, culture is considered as a system which again is divided into many ' sub-systems'. `Interaction between and among the sub-systems describes the change and continuity in a society. Fenfrew (1972) applied this systems theory model in the Aegean in connection with the emergence of civilization. In this culture change is not explained in terms of diffusion or adaptation but in terms of a multiplier effect. Even important aspects like environment, development, population growth etc. are not taken into consideration.

VI. World System Approach or Centre-Periphery Model

Wallersteinn (1974) developed this approach for the study of capitalism in Europe. Champion (1989:2-13) observes that "the kind of relationship (centre and periphery) typically analyzed in this way has been comparatively small scale, within a defined zone, whether that is geographical entity, such as an island or a river drainage or a historically defined polity, and focuses on a single central point, whether a small settlement in relation to the resources in its catchment area or a large urban centre in relation to his hinterland.

The application of this approach to the ancient cultures has been critically examined (Basa 1995). According to Rowlands (1987:51), "the exchange system of recapitalized societies was different from that of the capitalist ones since in the former case the form of exchange is more politically motivated and directed towards control over persons rather than the directed towards control over persons rather than the direct intervention in the technological conditions of production and commodity exchange". In the recent years, the world system perspective has been widely reviewed and applied in a broad sense by considering the ideological and cosmological aspects which were ignored by the earlier workers (Basa 1995). In world system perspective, trade is organized at three levels: pan-regional, regional and local. Thus, it contextualizes the 'centre-periphery' approach in archaeology. This approach is relevant to both varied landscapes and a single geographical region.

VII. Commercial Development Model

This approach emphasizes the economic growth, which results in specialization and exchange. When the economy spreads, it enables individuals to take the advantage of the benefits of specialization and exchange; there is an increase in social complexity (Parsons and Price 1971, Million 1973).

VIII. Ethnographic Model for Trade and Exchange

In order to transcend the limitations of archaeological evidence, archaeologists often depend on ethnographic data, which help bridge the gap between a living culture and archaeological remains. Ethnographic parallels are not only useful in identifying specific objects that are exchanged but also give ample evidence to deal with the associated data that are realistic in terms of actual behavior (Chang 1972). People living in diverse ecological and physiographic zones exploited resources and exchanged them with others for objects they did not posses. The exchange network takes place in two forms: (i) impersonal form of trade with little oral communication or close face to face contact that has been termed as 'silent trade' (Price 1980) and (ii) trade in general form. This trade also includes regional and inter-regional perspectives (a) Long distance type between traders from traders from state societies and people from primitive tribes, and (b) Short distance trade between traders from chiefdoms and tribes with the people from organized societies.

5.2 Literary and Inscriptional Evidences

5.2.1 Sangam Literature

The Sangam literature, an anthology of love and war poems in Tamil, serves as a primary source of information for the early historic period, which is otherwise called the Sangam Age of Tamilakam. The major works of the Sangam corpus are, Ettutogai (Eight Anthologies) and Paththupattu (Ten Idylls) collectively known as Pathinenmelkanaku (18 major works). The literature narrates the day-to-day life of people residing in five-different landscapes, namely Kurinji (the hilly zone), Mullai (pastoral zone), Marutam (the reverine zone), Zeytal (coastal zone) and Palai (the arid zone) as conceptualized by the poets. The first three centuries of the Christian Era is the widely accepted date for the composition of the Sangam Literature, though there are debates about the exact chronology. The Purananuru and Ahananuru are the most important Tamil poems referring to Roman trade. They make specific reference to Yavanas, who brought gold and wine to south

India, undoubtedly indicating that these Yavanas were Romans. We also know through other sources that gold and wine were among the chief commodities of export from Rome to India.

Yavanas were in great demand in ancient Tamil Nadu owing to their technical abilities as builders, carpenters and blacksmiths. Some of the Tamil kings even employed the Yavanas to produce sophisticated warfare, specially 'Siege engines'.

The Manimekalai (19, 107-108) mentions, artisans from distant northern kingdoms such as Avanti and Magadha. They worked with Yavanas to build the splendid city of Kaveripattinam or Puhar on the Coromandel Coast. The Silappadhikaram (5-10) mentions a Yavana settlement in this city.

The poem Mulleipattu (59062) alludes to the fact the Yavanas were strong and well-built, equipped with 'murderous swords', ignorant of the Tamil language and had no local sympathies, formed ideal gatekeepers or bodyguards in the palaces and forts of ancient Tamilakam.

The Tamil poems also refer to the Yavana lamp that was known for its steady flame without a flicker. Such lamps were in great demand in India. These exotic lamps were indeed a novelty to the Indians. The poem Perumbanatruppadai (311-319) refers to a Yavana lamp in the shape of a swan. Another poem named Nedunalvadei (101-103), describes a different variety of Yavana lamps crafted as statues of women, holding in their folded palms, the tahali or bowl to contain oil for lighting the lamp. These lamps are very similar to the pavai vilakku- a female figure, in metal, with a lamp in its hands – used in some homes and temples of Tamil Nadu to this day.

5.2.2 Western Accounts

The principal Graeco-Roman books dealing with the trade include Naturalis Historia or Natural History by Pliny (77AD), the Periplus Maris Erythraei (80-89 AD) and Geography by Claudius Ptolemy (150 AD). These Greco-Roman works are more useful than the Tamil poems not only because they provide more detailed and accurate descriptions of the trading networks and goods, but also because they are precisely datable. Thus, a comparative study of the information provided in these classical texts reveals a clear picture of the gradual development of the trade. These texts collectively confirm that trade slowly began on the Malabar Coast around the 2nd -1st centuries BC and steadily shifted to the Coromondal coast by the 1st century AD. Thus, while the perilous (1st century AD) provides limited information on the east coast of India, Ptolemy's Geography (2nd century AD) contains copious references to the Coromandel ports.

The most noteworthy Graeco-Roman work is the Perilous Maris Erythraea, which refers to the sea that included Read Sea, the Gulf of Aden and western Indian Ocean. It is believed to have primarily served as a guide book for ancient sailors of the Indian Ocean. The author of the Periplus was probably a Greek sailor who sailed from the ports of Red Sea to the western coast of India in the last decades of the 1st century AD. The book describes the routes from Red Sea to the western coast of India, and the major harbours and emporia including Muziris and the commodities of trade.

The lists of the items of trade in the Periplus corroborate and substantially add to the information provided by the Sangam Literature. As per the Perilous (56), the items imported into India included coins, topaz, coral, antimony, copper, tin, lead, crude glass, wine and wheat. Wheat was meant exclusively for the foreign merchants stationed in India. Among the exports from India to Rome were fine pearls, diamonds, sapphires, ivory, silk, spikenard, pepper and tortoise-shell.

Like the Perilous, Pliny's Natural History vividly describes certain trade commodities such as coral, beryl and pepper. He says that the beryl stones were found exclusively in India and were considered very valuable by the Roman (Naturalis Historia, XXXVII-XX 76, XXI 80). It seems European coral was as valuable to the Indians as the Indian pearls were to the Romans (Naturalis Historia, XXXII-XI21, 23). Pliny expresses surprise at the Roman attraction for the India pepper that has neither a sweet taste nor a pleasing appearance (Naturalis Historia, XII-XIV 26, 29).

Apart from the above major classical works, there are many more Greco-Roman evidences for the trade. The Roman emperor Tiberius, in a letter to Senate, castigated those who squandered their wealth on Indian gems (Annals of Tacitus, III. 53). Then, there is the story of the lady who took no care of her looks for her husband but saved up her Indian lotions and perfumes to impress her lovers (Satires VI, 464-66). The Tabula Peutingeriana or Peutingerian Tables (forth century AD?) records a temple for the Roman emperor Augustus at Muziris but no trace of the same exists on date A mid-2nd century AD. Papyrus from Vienna documents the shipment of around 700 to 1700 pounds of nard, 4700 pounds of ivory, and 790 pounds of textiles from Muziris to the African port of Alexandria.

Ancient Greek and Latin sources constitute the sole evidence for the exchange of embassies between the South Indian Kingdoms and Rome. Writers like Suetonius (first-second centuries AD), Lucius Annaeus Florus (Second century AD), Aurelius Victor (fourth century AD) and Paulus Orosius (fifth century AD) mention diplomatic missions sent by the kings of India to the Roman emperor Augustus in the years 25 BC and 20 BC one of the Indian envoys received by Augustus to have been from the Pandya Kingdom. Among the other Roman emperors to receive envoys from India were Traja (98-117 AD), Antoninus Pius (138-61 AD) and Constantine the Great (307-37AD). Constantine received ferocious animals and precious stones as gifts from the Indian ambassadors.

5.3. Trade and Trade Routes

5.3.1 Trade Routes in Tamil Nadu

It is widely accepted that trade is considered as one of the chief traits of state society. Trade played an important role in the territorial expansion during the early historic period. Exchange of commodities among the various places of Tamil Nadu as well as to other regions of South India were one of the factors responsible for the rise of commercial centers/ markets which later developed into urban centers (Fig. 14). Direct barter was a common mode of exchange as known from the literature (Purananuru 33:1-6). Rice and salt were popular in the barter trade 'as a common measure of value' because of their demand and storability (Singaravelu, 1966). The salt merchants travelled on their bullock carts exchanging salt for paddy (Ahananuru 140:7). Indirect evidence of exchange of goods is also available from the archaeological record. The occurrence of shell (Turbinella Pyrum), fish bones and cowrie (Moneta moneta) shells of marine origin in the interior regions of Tamil Nadu is a definite archaeological evidence for the exchange of goods (Selvakumar, 1996; cf. Smith, 2002:140-141). Trading was a profit-oriented activity and thus attracted the Paratavars, who were mainly fishermen and salt makers (Maloney, 1969), suggesting the participation of locals in the trade activities.

The variation in the landscape and the differential distribution of resources created a structural disparity that seems to have encouraged the trade and exchange activities. The development of interest for products of the hill region (vension and areca nut) in the coastal region and vice-versa (i.e. fish and salt from the coastal region) definitely shows active interaction among the various regions. Perhaps such a demand for a variety of goods among the regions required specialized traders. The term "vanikan" was used to denote traders and cattu to caravans. Traders moved in groups and employed yavanars (foreign bodyguards) for their protection from robbers. The Tamil-Brahmi inscriptions at Mangulam and Kodumanal refer to nigama (guild or corporate bodies) attesting the trading organizations. The alagarmalai inscription (in Madurai district) of the 1st century BC refers to salt merchant (uppa vanikan or umanar), Jaggery or toddy (?) trader (panita vanikan), and trader in ploughshare (kolu vanikan) (Mahadevan, 2003) as the donors of caves of heterodox sects. The Cirupanarrupadai mentions that the carts of salt traders traveled long distance for selling salt. Pattinappalai has a reference to paddy that came by boats moored at Kaveripattinam. The cities of Puhar and Madurai had very active markets known as angadis (Champakalakshmi, 1996 : 106). It appears that various groups right from the tribal of the bill areas to the fishermen of the coastal area participated in trade (Stiles, 1993; Gupta, 2002; Selvakumar, 2002) (see Table below). The extensive nature of the trade network is attested by the presence of fragments of Rouletted Ware and pottery with Tamil-brahmi inscriptions at the inland (rural) settlements of S. Pappinayakkapatti and T. Kallupatti in the Gundar Basin.

Table 3 : Specialized Traders of the Early Historic Period.

Item of Trade	Name of the Trader	Type of Evidence & Reference
Salt	Umanar or Uppu vanikam	Arch: Pottery from Uraiyur Ins: Algarmalai Inscriptions Lit: Cirupanarrupadai; Ahananuru 140
Jaggery/toddy (?)	Panita Vanikan	Ins: Alagarmalai and Pugalur
Ploughshare	Kolu Vanikan	Ins: Alagarmalai
Gold	Pon Vanikan/ponkolvan	Ins: Alagarmalai
Bead or Gem testers	Mani vannakkan	Ins: Alagarmalai and Pugular
Textile	Aruvai vanikan	Ins: Alagarmalai

(after Mahadevan 2003: 60 & 141)

Arch: Archaeological, Ins: Inscriptions, Lit: Literary

5.3.2 Long Distance Trade and Contacts

Trade and contacts with North India

The ancient Tamilakam in the beginning of the early historic period rose above the intra eco-zone trade to active inter-regional trade with other provinces of the subcontinent. This inter-regional trade must have begun much before the 1st century BC, when trade with the Mediterranean region commenced as attested by the presence of Rouletted Ware in the Pre-Arretine level at Arikamedu. More research is necessary to ascertain this. The Indian Ocean trade must have incorporated the already existing local trade networks and exchange systems. The evidence of NBPW from Alagankulam and Korkai, references to the pearls of the Pandyan country in the Koutilya's Arthasastra (Arunachalam, 1952), the possible source of Rouletted Ware-abundantly found at the coastal sites of Arikamedu and Alagankulam- being the Bengal origin, the presence of Tamil-Brahmi inscriptions with a mix prakrit words, concepts such as nigama, performances of sacrifice (e.g. Rajasuya) by the chieftains of the Sangam age, rock shelters with beds dedicated to the Jaina monks with inscriptions, bricks and tiles comparable in form and size to those from the North India, presence of the Mauryan punch marked coins, and Red Polished Ware sherds from Arikamedu and Kaveripattinam highlight contacts with the Deccan and the north. There must have been migration of people from North India, though one is not sure about the nature, intensity and the precise chronology of these migrations. Some of the traders perhaps migrated from North India and participated in trade activities. The terms such as Nigma and Visaki in the Tamil-Brahmi inscriptions at Kodumanal are taken to indicate the presence of merchants from Deccan and Andhra Pradesh (Champakalakshmi, 1996). There are references to 'vangam' as a type of ship and 'kalingam' as a type of cloth in the Sangam literature. It appears that 'kalingam' cloth was made in the Kalinga region. Does "vangam" refer to a type of boat made in Bengal?

Gogte (2002) argues for the colonization of the Coromandel coast by the traders from Bengal and political control based on the material culture evidence especially that of Rouletted Ware. How does the appearance of bricks and new types of pottery can be explained? Do these new material remains could have been introduced by the migrant traders, it is farfetched to assume that traders from Bengal single-handedly set-up and operated the ports and 'ruled substantial part of South India' without a critical analysis of the material remains and the historical processes. For example, there are references to the Chola king collecting duties on the commodities at Kaveripattinam (Pattinappalai 120-136), which is a clear evidence for the political control of the Cholas over the port. Similarly, Arikamedu/ Virampattinam was under the control of Thithan of Virai according to the literature.

5.3.3 Trade with the Mediterranean and East Asia

Long distance trade connected the Tamil country with the Mediterranean region and Southeast Asia through the Indian Ocean trade network (Warmington, 1974; Begley and De puma, 1991; Gupta, 1997; Rajan, 2002). The impact of the overseas trade was high in peninsular India, especially the Tamil country, since the direct sea-route to the Mediterranean region was very active after the 'discovery' of the monsoon winds by Hippalus (Fig.15). The luxury items such as Roman gold, silver, wine and table ware were imported and spices, beads of semiprecious stones and fine cloths were exported. The Greco-Roman texts and the discovery of coin hoards point to the large amount of gold that went to India because of pepper/spice trade. Amphorae, a jar used for importing wine and other commodities (garum sauce and olive oil) occur at many sites on the Coromandel Coast such as Vasavasamudram,

Kaveripattinam, Arikamedu, Alagankulam, Kudikadu and Korkai, and on the Malbar coast at Pattanam. Apart from Mediterranean pottery such as amphorae and Arretine (terra sigillata) found in India, the materials of Indian origin found at Jaffna in Sri Lanka, Beikthano in Burma (Thaw, 1968 : 64), Thailand (Shanmugam, 1993), Indonesia, Quseri-al-Qudim and Berenike on the Red Sea coast, Egypt (Tomber, 2000 : Mahadevan, 2003) attest to this trade. The Sinhalese-Brahmi inscriptions identified at Arikamedu, Alagankulam, Kaveripattinam and Kanchipuram point to strong foreign contacts. The Sangam literature mentions that people of Kaveripattinam could speak many languages, as numerous traders visited the port from various regions. The traders from all regions- Tamil country, Andhra, Sri Lanka and North India could have been involved in overseas trade. The distribution of Roman coins and other artefactual remains in the Tamil country suggest that the wealth generated through this trade was distributed among the local population. This trade must have been a major source of economic gain for the various groups involved in trade, since a definite increase in the variety of archaeological remains from the excavated sites is seen with the onset of this trade.

5.3.4 Overseas Trade at Arikamedu

The author of the Perilous mentions Poduke, believed to be Arikamedu, as one of the emporia on the Coromandel Coast, but he tells us very little about it or its trade. Imports from the Mediterranean, thus, are the primary source of information for understanding the history of maritime commerce at Arikamedu in particular and South India in general. Found at the site so far are fragments of shipping amphorae, cups and plates of terra sigillata, ceramic lamps and unguentaria, blue glazed faience and glass bowls, and perhaps gems. Most imported artifacts survive in very small fragments.

The most difficult of all questions is how to establish the identity of the traders and regulators of trade at Arikamedu. It has usually been taken for granted that the overseas trade was initiated and handled by Roman subjects. Greco-Roman involvement in the trade is almost certain from the finds. Furthermore, the pottery suggests that some westerners may have resided at Arikamedu on a long-terms basis, but whether they controlled all the flow of trade to the west is far from certain. From the finds it is difficult to gauge what the strength of the western population might have been at any given time, or what role the westerns might have played in the regulation of trade. On the other hand, it is evident that the architecture of Arikamedu is not Greco-Roman. The imported pottery, including amphorae, forms a mere 1% of the pottery of the site, and even pottery which seems to evolve from the western prototypes is small. The imports and derivatives from imports reflect the presence, perhaps needs, of westerners but not on a large scale.

The maritime route between the Mediterranean and Arikamedu or the Coromandel Coast in general, was probably through the Red Sea throughout the ancient period. Although, the Arabian-Persian Gulf route to the upper coast of western India is of great antiquity and was in use at the time of trade with Arikamedu, archaeological evidence so far does not indicate the extension of this route to the Coromandel Coast. The Red Sea route to south India, on the other hand, is very vividly described in the Periplus.

On the western end of the route, Alexandria and the Red Sea ports were points of transshipment of merchandise to and from the Mediterranean. The uncertain element is whether the Malabar ports were points of transshipment for the Coromandel Coast, particularly Arikamedu.

On the basis of a study of the Periplus, Lionel Casson in several of his most recent publications has proposed that western ships did not sail, at least on a regular basis, to the east coast of India. In order to reconcile the evidence of western presence at Arikamedu and Kaveripattinam with that of the Periplus he suggests that westerners residing on the east coast were middlemen chiefly engaged in forwarding goods to associates on Malabar Coast and not all the way to Egypt. W still do not fully understand the mechanisms of commerce between the Malabar and Coromandel coasts.

Moreover, recent analysis of sherds of "roulette ware" from Sembiran and Pacung in Bali and Arikamedu and Karaikadu on the Coromandel Coast suggests uniformity of source materials (Ardia et al. 1993). But where the points of distribution and redistribution of luxury ceramics were remain to be identified.

5.3.5 Coastal and Inland Trade at Arikamedu

Interconnecting the overseas trade were no doubt inland and coastal trade networks (Fig.19). To determine their extent we must rely primarily on the distribution of pottery, particularly fine wares. Dishes of what is commonly known as "roulette ware" are the most extensively distributed of all types of pottery found at Arikamedu. Briefly stated, its presently known distribution extends over most of the eastern coast, from Chandraketugarh and Tamluk in the north of east coast to Alagankulam and Periyapattinam in the south, and to Mantai and Kantarodai on the Sri Lankan coast. Inland it has been reported from Anuradhapura in inland Sri Lanka, from various locations in Tamil Nadu and Andhra Pradesh, mostly in the plains of the Krishna and Kaveri Basins. Occasional sherds are reported from sites in Maharashtra and Uttar Pradesh as well; these most probably traveled on routes along the rivers of the Godavari and the Ganga drainage systems. Thus, the distribution of "roulette ware" shows that the pottery or its technology was traded from a place of original manufacture. It also appears that one network on which " rouletted ware" traveled was all along the eastern sea board, including Sri Lanka; the other networks interconnected with the interior. Another fine ware vessel form, first identified at Arikamedu (Wheeler et.al.1946:

Type 19), is a bowl with stamped figurative motifs. This bowl form seems also to have traveled on the coastal route, but in small quantity and to a limited number of destinations. In the case of coarse wares, the situation might be somewhat different. A few of the distinctive vessel forms first identified at Arikamedu have parallels elsewhere; these may represent a different type of trade. Distribution of certain other coarse ware forms, such as jars with perforations, or jars/bowls with paddle impressed decoration, may also reveal short or long distance trade. Of all the graffiti at Arikamedu which can be read, only a few (Wheeler et.cal;, 1946: Fig 476, Nos. 15 and 20; and fig. 5.21 here) refer to the ownership of the vessel. In all three cases, the profile is of a "rouletted ware" rim profiles.

Turning to other types of information, most of the raw materials for lapidary at Arikamedu must have come from the inland region, travelling perhaps on the same routes as ceramic fine wares, through the Krishna and Godavari River valleys. Inland communication networds between the eastern and western parts of the extreme south apparently intersected at major metropolitan centers, such as Uraiyur and Karur, where ceramics and other products from different regions seem to overlap (Begley 1983: 480).

Therefore, other crafts, craft technologies, or simply ideas may have travelled on these routes as well. Line that the presence of several lapidary wasters from earlier excavations suggesting the existence of a local industry which may have Western inspired. So what else traveled on these routed, archaeology does not clarify as yet; a variety of merchandise ranging from staples to luxury items could have been traded, some no doubt for or from the overseas market as well.

5.3.6 Items of Local and Regional Exchange on the Subcontinent

The archaeological record permits us to examine the variety of manufactured and traded items within the Indian subcontinent. The

Pyramidal diagram indicates three types of trade goods found in Indian Archaeological sites of the early historical period (Monica L. Smith 2002).

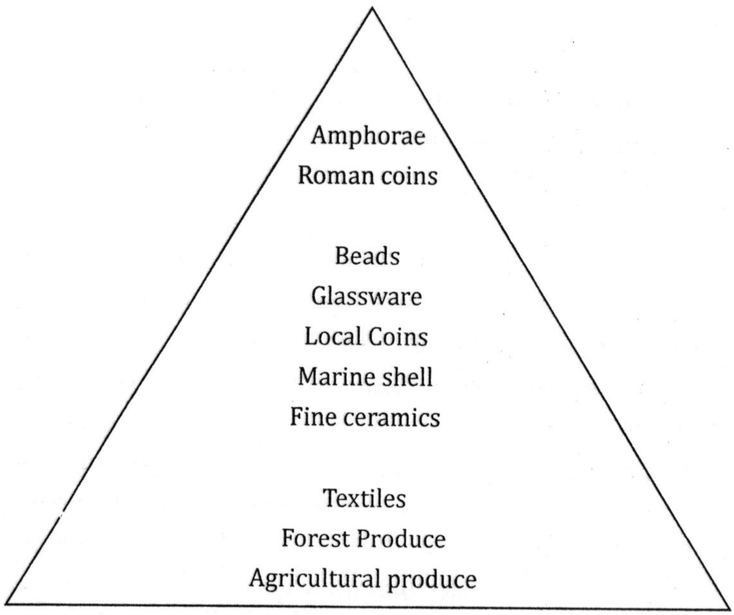

Products are listed at the top of the 'pyramid' being the rarest and represent exotic products arriving in the subcontinent as a result of Indian Ocean trade. The goods in the middle category are those found at almost all sites of the early historic period in India, and which are derived from local raw materials. The final category represents the types of goods which probably constituted the largest proportion of inland trade.

These goods were traded between sites for domestic use, but also became part of the long-distance trade network, because items such as forest products and agricultural products were desired goods for overseas trade. However, these goods are perishable, so only indirect evidence of the production and consumption of these goods is usually found in archaeological sites. The most likely items to be found archaeologically are located in the middle category, consisting durable goods whose distribution appears to be limited to the Indian subcontinent. Excavation reports from Early Historic sites throughout India consistently list a common catalog of items such as marine shells, ornaments, fine ceramic and coins. The widespread appearance of the same types of artifacts is due to two factors: the transfer of actual items, and the transmission of ideas and styles (Monica L. Smith 2002).

One particularly striking proof of the exchange of material items throughout the subcontinent in this period is found in the use of marine shells. The large gastropod Turbinella Pyrum has a natural distribution on the southeastern and northwestern coasts of the subcontinent (Nagappan Nayar and Mahadevan : 1974). However, it is found in many inland sites of Early Historic Period, in both whole and fragmentary form. The discovery of shell fragments far inland indicates that whole shells were transported rather than the fragile bangles; because the shell is quite distinctive, it is easy to recognize fragmentary portion in the archaeological record. As the shells of the minimum appropriate size for making bangles represent at least 150g, we can begin to see that regional exchange was not limited to very small items. The recovery of marine shells in the interior of the subcontinent indicates the transfer of both raw materials and technology and expertise, since the manufacturer of bangles from the shell requires skills in breaking the interior of the shell, and in sawing the upper rounded portion of the shell into bangles (Kenoyer 1983).

Other types of ornaments, such as beads and ear spools, were also widespread in the Early Historical period. The existence of prevailing bead styles indicates that both beads and information about fashion circulated in the inland trade networks. Beads made from rare or distant raw materials, such as lapis lazuli and carnelian, are sometimes recovered. At the same time, a consistent style of beads is noted from materials which are widely available, such as agate and freshwater shell. The presence of unfinished beads at many Early Historical sites suggests that beads were locally made, perhaps because the grinding and polishing of stone beads was a labour intensive but not particularly a skilled task.

Another indicator of flourishing trade in the subcontinent is found in the use of coins. As with the appearance of ornaments, the widespread distribution of coins indicates several levels of exchange activity, in the trade of physical coins as well as the understanding of the concept of coinage as facilitator of trade (Monica L. Smith 2002).

Other types of goods, such as ceramics, also provide evidence for the widespread distribution of prevailing styles as well as the transfer of actual objects. Many sites of the early historic period contain well-made ceramics, such as the Red Polished Wares recovered at many sites in the western subcontinent, and Rouletted Wares primarily distributed on the eastern coasts of India (for maps of distribution, see Fig. 11). V. Begley characterizes Rouletted Ware as being entirely different from the fine wares of the western coast, with a very limited range of styles in fabric. This is predominantly gray pottery (Begley 1991). The only shape in which this ware is found is a flat-bottomed dish with a distinctive pattern of concentric circular bands of tiny indentations in the interior (Krishna Deva in Wheeler et.al. 1946: 45). These wares have gained importance not only because they are distinctive and well manufactures, but also because of speculations that they were either direct Mediterranean imports, or made in the subcontinent in imitation of Mediterranean wares(e.g. Subbarao 1953; Begley 1991, 1994).

Moreover, the archaeological evidence from the subcontinent indicates that many types of goods were manufactures, both from locally-available materials (such as clay in the making of ceramic vessels) and from non-local materials (as seen by marine-shell debris fround hundreds of kilometers inland). In the analysis of early trade routes through which goods were transported, the identification of the production strategies utilized in the manufacture of finished products is as important as the identification of the raw materials used. The production of items for local and regional exchange within the subcontinent was the result of a variety of manufacturing techniques. The archaeological record provides evidence for specialized manufacture in items such as shell bangles and metal coins, where the manufacture of finished items could have been accomplished by single individuals or small teams.

Evidence for the large-scale manufacturing of goods in this period is limited, though it appears that the concept of the large-scale organization of production was recognized as indicated by inscriptions which mention 'guilds' as donors to religious institutions (Ray 1986). The traders/guilds mentioned in the early and medieval Tamil literature include weavers, potter, bamboo-workers, bead maker and salt seller (Ray 1985). The presence of what appears to be organized corporate bodies identified as makers of particular goods or holding market specialties indicated that certain craft activities were carried out on a scale surplus production areas. At the same time, there is also evidence for relatively unskilled and repetitive labour, such as that utilized in the manufacture of beads. The use of unskilled labour is also implied in the many mundane steps of the production process of ceramics, terracotta and clay ornaments: acquisition of fuel and clay, initial preparation of raw materials, and transportation of finished products. Many of the trade items documented by the historical and archaeological record, including textiles and agricultural commodities, could have been produced at the household level utilizing the family labour. Households would have engaged in trade directly, through barter or sale, and may also have seen the results of their production pooled for exchange by guilds and merchants acting as middlemen.

CHAPTER SIX

DISCUSSION AND CONCLUSION

Archaeological and historical evidence indicates that towns and villages in Early Historic India were the focal-points of a very active trading environment. Any site could participate in trade through the production of some kind of tradable surplus, such as agricultural produce, raw materials, or finished products. At the same time, these towns and villages were stopping-points along the routes of travel for pilgrims, traders, and political figures. The recent surveys carried out at Arikamedu enable us to assess the extent to which local exchange was a significant component of economic activity. For Arikamedu, the earliest period of its history – from around the third century BC to the second century AD – is the most eventful and important. According to these recent surveys it is inferred that prior to the advent of the Roman trade, Arikamedu was one among the scores of Megalithic or Iron Age settlements in South India. These settlements are characterized by the use of iron tools and implements, different types of pottery and elaborate stone burials. But one should remember that unlike most other Megalithic sites, clear evidences for Megalithic graves, so far, not been discovered at Arikamedu.

Many of the Megalithic settlements including Arikamedu were located close to rivers that enabled transport and communication, through boats, with other sites in the region. Indeed, it is further inferred that some of these settlements were deliberately located along local trade routes. In some places, the Megalithic culture continued even after the commencement of the Rome-India trade. This is proved by the discovery of Roman coins buried, along with various household goods, within Megalithic graves in the Coimbatore region of Tamil Nadu.

The region around Arikamedu abounds in Megalithic sites such as Sengamedu, Parikal, Tiruvakarai and Suttukeni. At Suttukeny (a nearest rich Megalithic site) a four-holded gold spacers were recovered. A similar type of object was also found during V.Begley's excavation (in1992) in Arikamedu at early level (Pl.63). There is adequate archaeological evidence to show that Arikamedu had trade and cultural links with many Megalithic and Early Historic settlements in the region. Thus, Arikamedu's position as a prominent trade centre appears to have been established even prior to the commencement of the Rome-India Trade. The Romans chose this place as their trading station on account of its strategic location close to the sea and the firm links that it had with the hinterland.

During the period of Roman trade, Arikamedu was, again, one among several Coromandel Coast trading ports frequented by the Roman traders. Such ports include Vasavasamudram, Karaikadu, Kaveripattinam, Alagamkulam and Korkai. Arikamedu was the largest and most important among all these ports. Here, besides Roman's Rouletted wares, there are limited/inferior/locally made rouletted potteries are also reported from interior sites of Arikamedu which are contemporary to Roman phase. Within Tamil Nadu there are at least 60 sites revealing this pottery tradition, reported both from excavations and surface collections. While considering the remarks of Begley who mentions that "Rouletted pottery occurs only in urban and religious centers", the occurrence of the inland Rouletted Ware sites deserves an explanation. Besides its connections with hinterland sites such as Kottaimedu on the banks of the river Pambai, Manikolai, Tirusopuram (for their beads manufacturing and selling) and the recently discovered sites in the study region, Arikamedu also occasionally interacted with some of the other ports such as Vasuvasamudram, Karaikudu and Kaveripattinam.

Regarding the source of raw material for lapidary work at Arikamedu they must have come from the interior sites traveling perhaps on the same routes as ceramic fine wares, through the Krishna and Godavari doab. The beds of these two rivers also yielded jasper, agates, and possibly even prase (Francis 2002:116-118). Ingredients for the glassmakers of Arikamedu also came from the doab as this region was under-populated and underdeveloped at this time and with in the area Leshnik (1974: 19-20) called the "Tribal Belt". Further, the raw materials were moved to the two sites of Arikamedu and Kodumanal (rich megalithic site from Erode district). From Arikamedu, these raw materials must have reached to satellite sites like Manikolai and Thirusopuram where the recent survey exposed humpty numbers of glass beads besides conical jar fragments.

In the present area Rajan has identified many megalithic habitation sites with engraved Jain caves in the South Arcot region (see Fig.20), which will ultimately help us to identify of ancient trade routes. For example, the strategic location of Tirukoyilur and landmark inscription of Athiyaman (ruler of Tagadur, modern Dharmapuri region) at Jambai (in Villupuram district) are suggestive of well-organized trade network extending from Marandahalli (Kolar region), Uttangarai, Chengam, Thirukoyilur, Jambailinking Sengamedu with Arikamedu (Fig.18). A recent re-survey conducted by the present author on Sengamedu, near Vridhachalam taluk of Villupuram district, helped that the site Sengamedu shared lot with Arikamedu and most probably acted as small reverine port to Arikamedu. Particularly those massive structures found at Sengamedu seem to be like area warehouse at Arikamedu.

The above study may thus conclude that both prior to and during the period of Roman trade, south eastern India had a large trading network of coastal and inland ports and market centers that were intimately linked with Arikamedu. During the height of the Roman trade, the smaller hinterland centers provided the goods and services including agricultural products needed by the large and busy urban settlement of Arikamedu. Thus, these smaller sites emerged as satellite centers around Arikamedu. Following these latest researches on Arikamedu, debate has now started among these schools over the inland transshipment of commodities that reached Arikamedu for export purpose, and the imported commodities of Arikamedu that distributed to the inland urban centers. Paradoxically, it has been concluded that the imported goods were fully consumed by the Arikamedu settlers and all the exported goods were produced from Arikamedu and surrounding area. Generally the size of these sites ranges from 5-50 acres, and show some sort of hierarchy between them. And presence of more sites in Pambai valley also suggests that inland transshipment was not only carried along the river Gingee but it was also in the banks of Pambai beyond Suttukeni and Tiruvakkarai.

So the present research work on satellite settlements of Arikamedu urge us the necessity of the identification of strategic location of Arikamedu in the context of Megalithic exchange system and their interaction with the other early historical sites including North India. The identification can be possible only by further extensive exploration/ excavation in and around Arikamedu including (old) South Arcot region of Tamil Nadu.

It is only in the context of these that the dynamics of growth and expansion of satellite settlements of Arikamedu can be comprehended.

BIBLIOGRAPHY

Aiyappan, A. 1941. A Dakshina Taxila, Historic Relief from Arikamedu. The Hindu, March 23.

Antony, F.C., ed. 1982. Gazetteer of India, Union Territory of Pondicherry, 2 vols. Pondicherry: Administration of Union Territory of Pondicherry.

Ardika, I.W. and P.S. Bellwood 1991. "Sembiran: the beginnings of Indian contact with Bali". Antiquity 65:221-232.

Banerjee, N.R., 1956. The Excavations at Sengamedu, in March of India, Vol.8, New Delhi.

Baliga. B.S. 1961. Madras District Gazetteer, South Arcot by State Edutor, District Gazetteers, Egmore, Chennai pp. 10-122.

Begley, V. 1983 "Arikamedu Reconsidered". American Journal of Archaeology 87: 461-481.

______, 1986 "Rouletting and Chattering, Decoration on Ancient and Present Day pottery in India". Expedition 28. 1:47-54.

______, 1988 "Rouletted ware at Arikamedu: A New Approach". American Journal of Archaeology.

______, 1991 "Ceramic Evidence for Pre-Periplus Trade on the Indian Coasta". In V. Begley and R.D. DePuma, eds. Rome and India: The Ancient Sea Trade. Madison: The University of Wisconsin Press.

______, 1993 "New Investigations at the port of Arikamedu". Journal of Roman Archaeology 6:93-108.

Begley, V. and R.D. DePuma, eds. 1991, Rome and India: The Ancient Sea Trade. Madison: University of Wisconsin Press. 155-196.

Berghaus, P. 1992 "Three Denari of Terius from Arikamedu in India". In D.W. Mac Dowellet al. eds. Indian Numismatics. History, Art and Culture. Essays in Honour of P.L. Gupta, Vol.l.l. Agam Indological Series 14: Delhi: Agam Kala Prakasham: 95-98.

Carswell, J. and M. Prickett 1984 "Mantai 1980: A Preliminary Investigation". Ancient Ceylon 5: 3-68.

Casal, J.M 1949 Fouilles de Virampatnam-Arikamedu. Paris: Imprimerie Nationale.

Casal, J.M and G. Casal 1956 Site urbain et funeraires des environs de Pondicherry. Paris: Press Universitaires de france.

Casson, L. 1980 "Rome's Trade with the East: The Sea Voyage to Africa and India". Transactions of the American Philosophical Association 110: 21-36.

_____, 1988 b "Rome's Maritime Trade with Eastern Coast of India". Cahires d' Histoire XXXIII.3-4: 303-308.

Charvat, P. 1993 "External contacts of Srilanka in the 1st millennium A.D". Archiv Orientalni 61: 13-29.

Chang, K.C. 1962. A Typology of Settlement and community pattern in some circumpolan societies, Arctic Anthropology 1:22-41.

Chang, K.C. 1972. Settlement Patterns in Archaeology, An Addition-Sirley Moduules in Anthropology No.24.

Comfort, H. 1991 "Teera Sigillata Arikamedu". In V. Begley and R.D. De Puma, des. Rome and India: The Ancient Sea Trade. Madison : The University of Wisconsin Press. 134-150.

Champakalakshmi, R., 1975-76. Archaeology and Tamil Literary Tradition. Puratattva 8:110-122.

Champakalakshmi, R, 1996. Trade, Ideology and Urbanization, New Delhi.

Chelliah, J.V. 1946. Pattapattu: Ten Tamil Idylls. Colombo: General Publishers Limited.

Deraniyagala, N. 1985 "The Citadal of Anuradhapura: Gadige 1984, a Preliminary Report". Ancient Ceylon 6:39-47

Devashayam, N. 1985 "Roman Jewellary from Vellalore site during the Sangam period". Lalit Kala 21:53.

Erdosy, G. 1988. Urbanization and Early Historic India : Oxfort: British Archaeological Report.

Francis, P. 1976-80: Some observations on the glass beads of Arikamedu". Revue Historque de Pondicherry XIII: 156-161.

______, 1991 "Bead making at Arikamedu and beyond". World Archaeology 23.1; 28-43.

Gazda, E.K. 1987 Chapter IV. The port and Description of the Extant Remains and Sequence of Construction". In A.M. Mc Cann, et al.eds., The Roman port and Fishery of Cosa.... A centre of Ancident Trade. Princeton University Press. 74-97.

Garstin, J.H. 1876. Dolmens of the Coromandal coast, Indian Antiquary 5: 159.

Garstin, J.H. 1878 Manual of the South Arcot District, Part II. Pp: 173-199.

Gurukkal, Rajan, 1989. Forms of production and forces of change in ancient Tamil Society, Studies in History 5 (2): 159-175.

Hornell, J. 1942 "The Chank Shell Cult of India". Antiquiry 16:113-133.

Indian Archaeology: A Review, New Delhi : Archaeological Survey of India.

Kasinathan, N. 1992 Alagankulam: a preliminary report. Madras: Tamil Nadu State Department of Archaeology.

Kasinatha, Natana & Majeed, Abdul., 1996. Thirukoyilur Excavation. Madras.

Krishnamurthy, R. 1985 Sangakala Cholar Nanayankal. Madras; R. Krishnamurthy.

______, 1987 Pandiyar Peruvaluthi Nanayankal. Madras : R. Krishnamurthy.

______, 1992 "Makkaotai Coins". In A.V.Narasimha Murthy ed., Studies in South Indian Coins 2. South Indian Numismatic Society. Madras : New era Publisher.

Lal B.B. 1968 "Examination of Rod of Glass- like materials from Arikamedu". Ancient India 14:139-143.

Mahadevan, I. 1968 "Corpus of the Tamil – Brahmi Inscriptions", In R. Nagaswamy ed. Seminor on Inscriptions 1996. Madras: Books (India) Private Ltd. 57-73.

______, 1970 " The ancient name of Arikamedu". In N. Subrahmanian, ed., Paritimar Kalainjar Nurrantu Vila Malar, V.K. Suryanarayana Sastri Century volume. Madurai. 204-206.

______, 1986 "An old Singhalese inscription from Arikamedu". Journal of the Asiatic Society of Bombay 56-59 (1981-84): 222-226.

Maloney, C. 1985 "Archaeology of South India: Accomplishment and prospects". In B. Stein ed. Essays on South India (Asian studies at Hawai. 15). Honolulu: University of Hawai Press. 1=40.

Margabandhu, C. 1985 Archaeology of Satavahana-Kshatrapa Times. Delhi: Sundeep Prakashan.

Makkhanlal, 1984. Settlement History and Rise of Civilization in the Ganga-Yamuna Doab from 1500 BC to 300 AD. Delhi : B.R. Publishing Corporation.

Mohanty, P. 1989. Mesolithic Settlement system of the Keonjhar District Orissa. Unpublished Ph.D. Dissertation. University of Poona, Pune.

Morrison, K.D. 1997. Commerce and Culture in South Asia: Perspectives from Archaeology and History. Annual Review of Anthropology 26: 87-108.

Nanda, S.C. 1984. Stone Age Cultures of Indravati Basin, Koraput District, Orisssa. Unpublished Ph.D. Dissertation. University of Poona, Pune.

Nagaswamy R. 1970 "Excavation at Korkai, District Tirunelveli". Damilica 1:50-54.

_____, 1981 a "Asoka and the Tamil Country: a new link". The Indian Express Sunday Magazine, Madras, 6th December 1981.

_____, 1981 b "Roman Sites in Tamil Nadu: Recent Discoveries". In M.S.Nagarajarao ed. Madhu: Recent Researches in Indian Archaeology and History (M.S. Deshpande festschrift). Delhi: Agam Kala Prakashan. 337-339.

_____, 1991 "Alagankulam: An Indo-Roman Trading Port", In C. Margabandhu et al. eds. Indian Archaeological Heritage, K.V. Soundra Rajan Festschrift, Vol.l Delhi' Agam Kala Prakashan. 247-254.

_____, 1995. Roam Karur, Madras.

Nambirajan, M., 2001, Recent Explorations in Ginger Taluk, Tamil Nadu. In Prof. Y Subbarayalu Felicitation Volume, Veliyittakam, Chennai, Pp 273-76

Pappu, S. 1996. Pleistocene Environment and Stone Age Adaptions in the Kortallayer Basin, Tamil Nadu. Unpublished Ph.D Dissertation. Deccan College, Pune.

Rajan, K, 1994. Archaeology of Tamil Nadu (Kongu Country), New Delhi.

_____, 1996. Archaeological Vazetteer of Tamil Nadu, New Delhi.

———, 1998. Archaeology of the South Arcot Region with special reference to Megalithic Burial Complexes, Man and Environment XXIII (1): 93-105.

———, 2002. Maritime Activities of the Tamils, in Man and Environment, Pune.

———, 2002. Recent Advances in Early Historic Archaeology of Tamil Nadu, in Kaveri (Y. Subbarayalu Feliciation Volume) pp.229-247, Chennai.

Ragava Iyengar, M. 1964. Velir Varalaru, (first ed 1913). Madras: Valluvar Pannai.

Rajavelu & Tirumurti, 1995. Tamizhnattut Tolliyal Agazhaivugal, Madras

Rajesh, M and Arun Raj, T. 2003. Some observations on Sengamedu-A hinterland Trade Centre of Arikamedu. CIAA Newsletter 17:17-25.

Ramachandran, K.S. 1980 Archaeology of South India, Tamil Nadu. Delhi: Sundeep Prakashan.

Raman, K.V. 1972 Some Aspects of Pandya History. Madras : Madras University.

———, 1988 Excavations at Uraiyur (Tiruchirappalli) 1965-69. Madras University.

———, 1991 "Further Evidence of Roman Trade Coastal Sites in Tamil Nadu". In V. Begley and R.D. De Puma eds. Rome and India: The Ancient Sea Trade. Madison : The University of Wisconsin Press. 125-133.

Ramaswamy, K., R. Balasubramanian, G. Chandrasekaran 1976-80 " Archaeomaganetic study of some excavations in Tamil Nadu". Revue Historique de Pondicherry 13: 186-90.

Ramaswamy et. Al., 1992. The Phenomenon of River Migration in Northern Tamil Nadu-Evidence from Satellite Data, Archaeology and Tamil Literature, In Man and Environment, Pune.

Raschke, M.g. 1978 "New Studies in Roman Commerce with the Esat". Aufstieg and Niedergang der romischen Welt 2.9.2:604-1378.

Ray, H.P., 1991. East Coast trade in Peninsular India C.200 B.C. to A.D.400., in South Asian Archaeology, Berlin

______, 1995. A Resurvey of Roman contacts with the East, in Athens, Aden, Arikamedu, New Delhi.

______, 2002. The Archaeology of Early Historic Maritime India, In Indian Archaeology in Retorspect. Archaeology & Historiography, Vol IV, New Delhi.

Ravi Chandran, 1998. Early (Iron Age) Settlements in Pondicherry Region, Un Published Report submitted to the Pondicherry Government.

Rice, P.M. 1987. Pottery Analysis : A Source Book. Chicago: The University of Chicago Press.

Robinson, H.A. 1959. Pottery of the Roman Period. (The Athenian Agora 5). Princeton : American School of Classical Studies at Athens.

Rouse, I. 1972. Settlement Patterns in Archaeology, in Man, Settlement Patterns in Archaeology, In Man, Settlement and Urbanism, Pp. 95-113. London.

Salomon, R. 1991. "Epigraphic Remains of Indian Traders in Egypt". Journal of the American Oriental Society III.4:731-736

Seneviratne, S. 1993. From Kudi to Natu: A suggested framework for the study of Pre-state political formations in early Iron age South India. The Sri Lankan journal of Humanities 19 (1&2): 57-77.

Sidebotham, S.E. 1991. "Ports of the Red Sea and the Arabia _ India trade". In V. Begley and R.D De Puma eds. Rome and India : The Ancient Sea Trade. Madison: The University of Wisconsin press 204-215.

Slane, K.W. 1991 " Observations on Mediterranean Amphoras and Tablewares Found in India". In V. Begley and R.D. De Puma eds. Rome and India: The Ancient Sea Trade. Madison. The University of Wisconsin Press. 204-215

Sopundara, a. 1987 "Studies in the Neolithic Culture in Tamil Nadu-Kerala: An Appraisal". Tamil Civilization 5.2: 34-47.

Soundara Rajan, K.V., 1994. Kaveripattinam Excavations 1963-73 A Port City on the Tamilnadu Coast, New Delhi.

Stern, E.M. 1991. "Early Roman Export Glass in India". In V. Begley and R.D.De Puma eds. Rome and India: The Ancient Sea Trade. Madison: The University of Wisconsin Press.

Subbrayalu, Y. 1984 "Vallam Excavations". Tamil Civilization 2.4:9-98.

Subrahmanya Aiyer, K.V. 1924 " The earliest monuments of the Pandya Country and their inscriptions". Proceedings of the Third Oriental Conference (Madras) 275-300

Suresh, S., "Roman Coins From Tamil Nadu". SSIC, 1992, Pp 19-34.

Trigger, B.G. 1967. Settlement Archaeology- Its Goals and Promises, American Antiquity 32: 149-160.

Venkatasubramanian, T.K. 1988. Environment and Urbanization in Early Tamilakam. Thanjavur, Tamil University.

Walker, M.J. and S. Santoso 1977 "Romano – Indian Rouletted Pottery in Indinesia". Asian Perpectives 20.2: 228-235.

Wallerstein, T. 1974. The world system: Capitalist agriculture and the origins of the European Economy in the sixteenth century, Newyork: Academic Press.

Wheeler, R.E.M. 1951 "Roman contact with India, Pakistan and Afganistan". In W.E.Grimes, ed. Aspects of Archaeology in Britain and Beyond. Essaya Presented to O.G.S. Crawford, London: H.W.Edwards. 354-381.

______, 1954 Rome Beyond the Imperial Frontiers. London: George Bell and Sons.

Wheeler, R.E. M, et al. 1946. "Arikamedu, an Indo-Roman Trading-station on the East Coast of India". Ancient India 2:17-125.

Will, W.<. 1987 "The Roman Amphoras". In A.M. Mccann et al. The Roman Port and Fishery of Cosa. Princeton University Press: 170-220.

Willey, G.R. 1955. Prehistoric Settlement patterns in the Viru Valley, Peru, Bureau of American Ethnology Bulletin p. 155.

Wirth, L. 1938, Urbanism as a way of life. American journal of Sociology, 44, No.1 July.

Zvelbil, K. 1956 "The Yavanas in Old Tamil Literature". Charisteria Orientation. Praha. 401-409.

INDEX

N

O

P

FIGURES

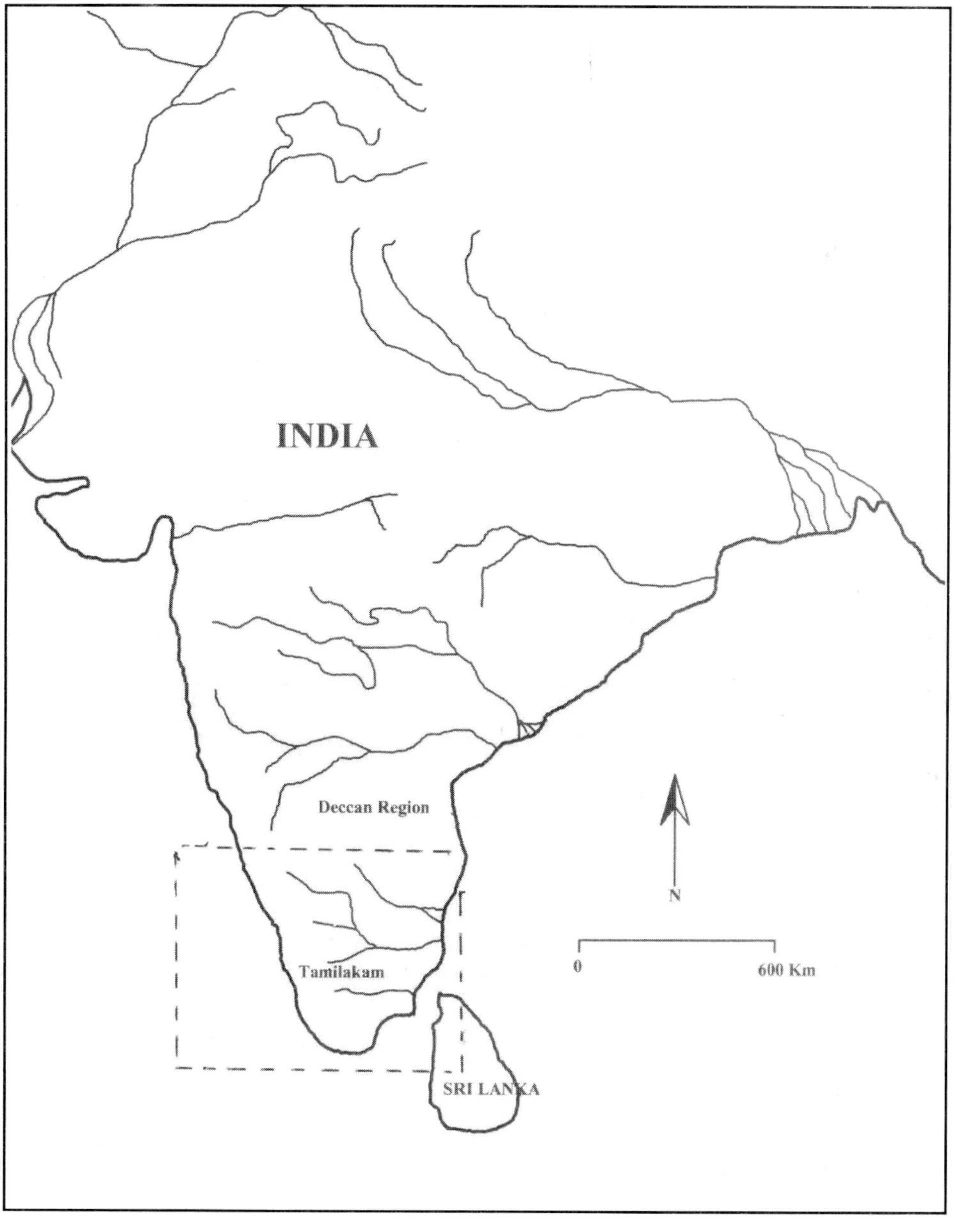

Fig. 01 : Map showing Ancient sites in Tamil Nadu.

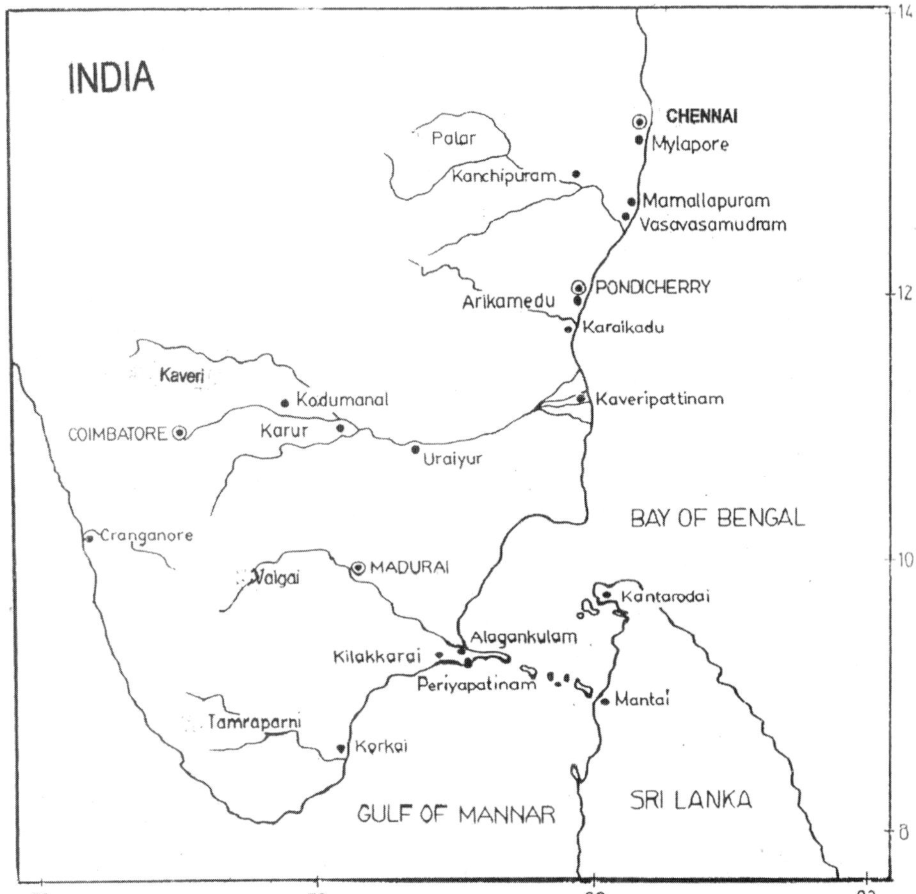

Fig. 02 : Map of South India: Arikamedu in Related ancient Sites.

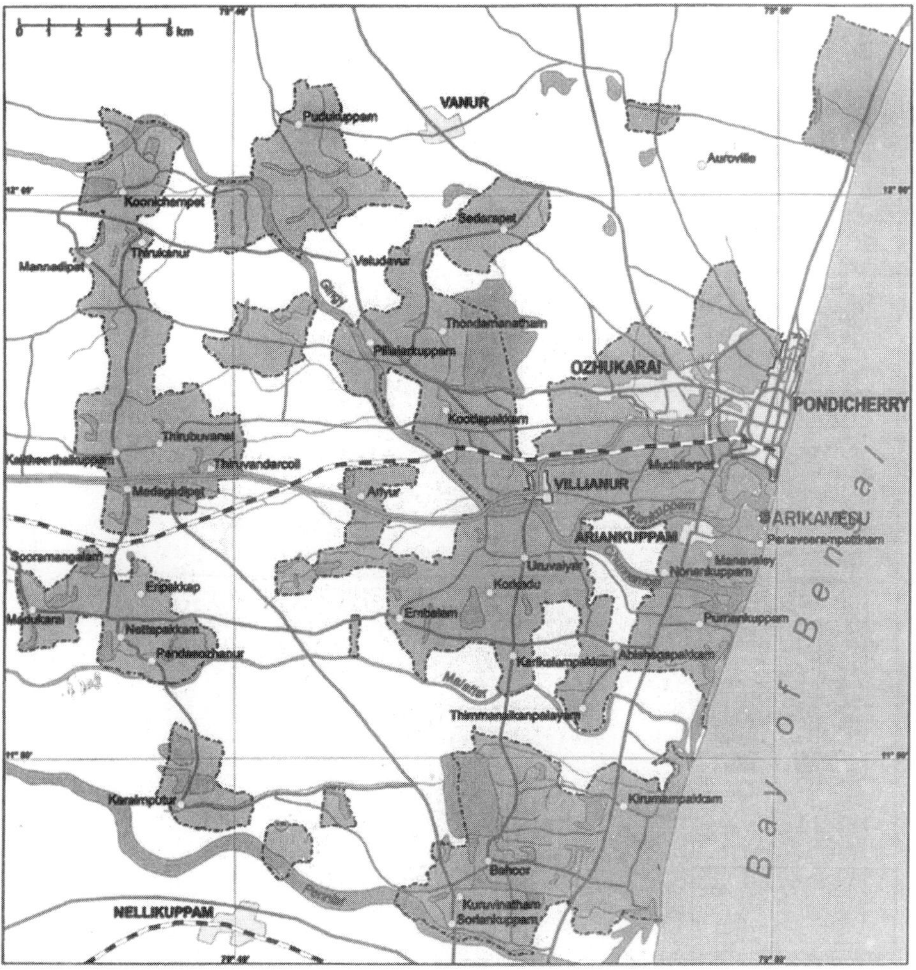

Fig. 03 : Map showing plan of Pondicherry.

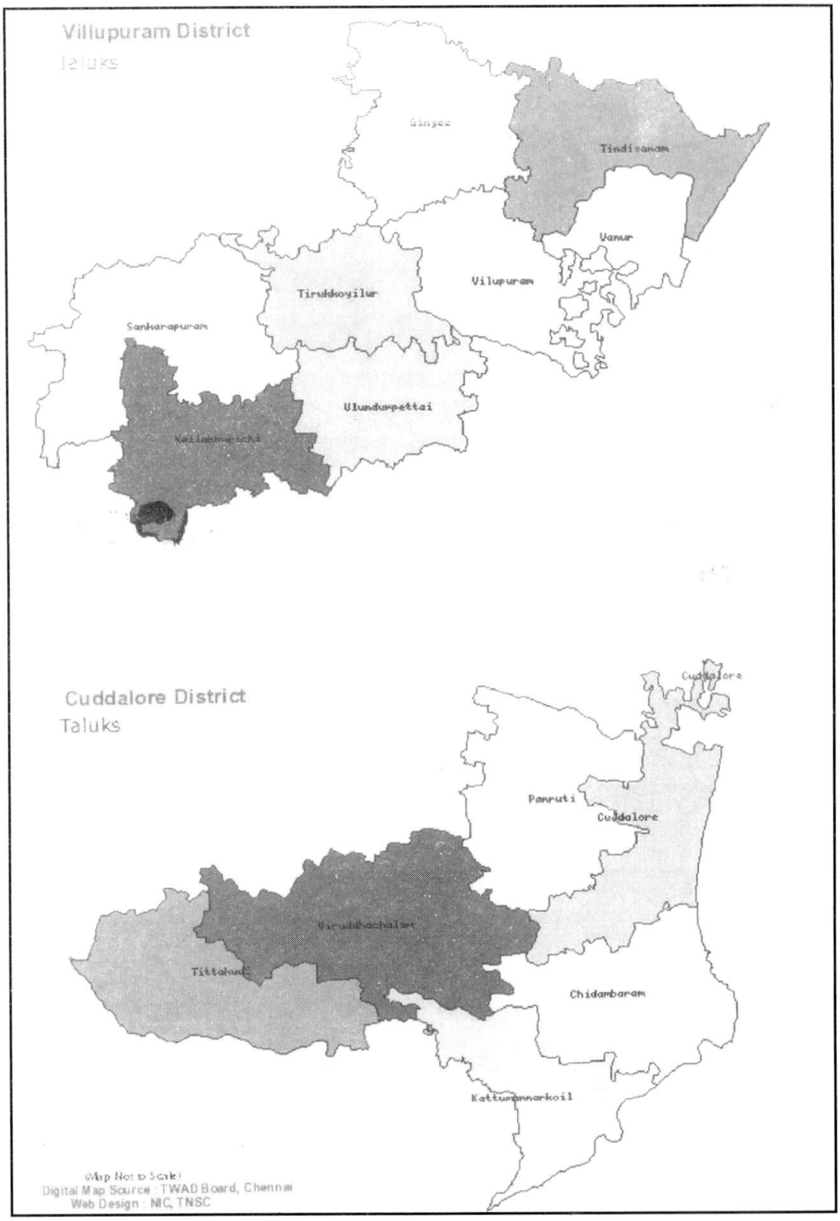

Fig. 04 : Map showing taluks of Villupuram and Cuddalore District (South Arcot region).

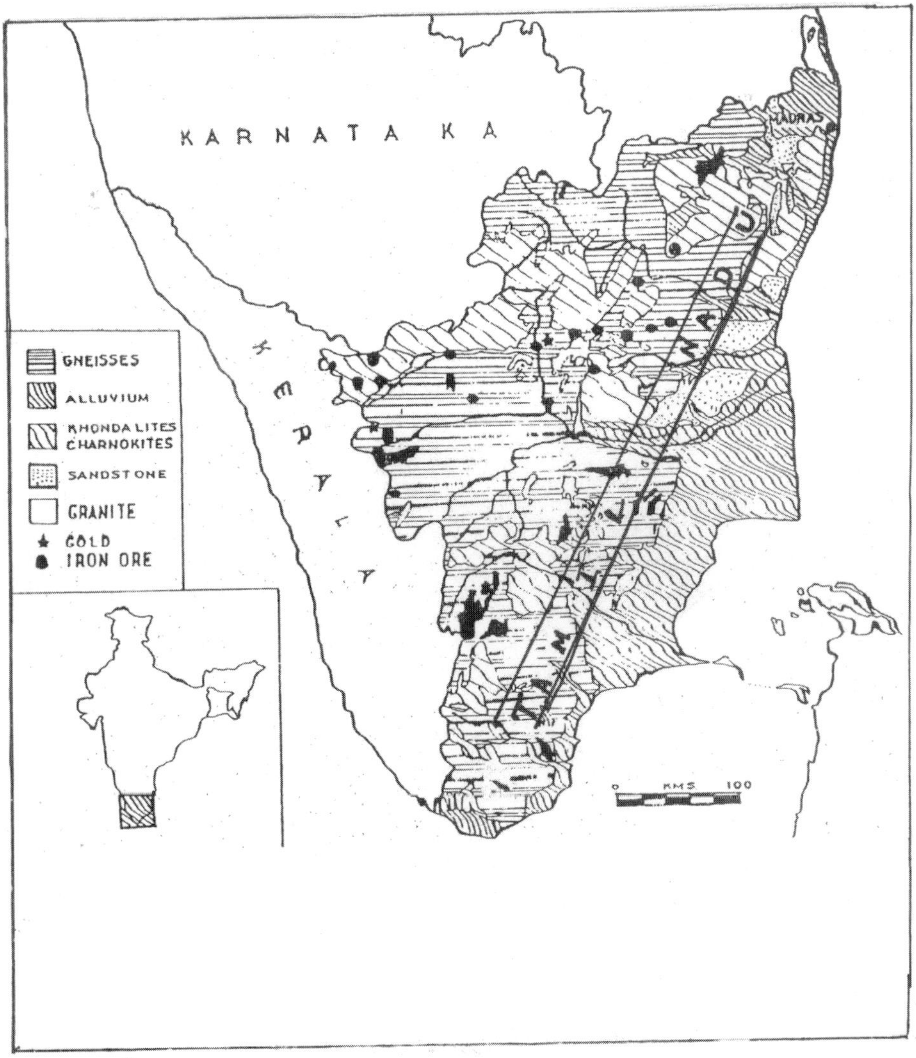

Fig. 05 : Geological Map of Tamil Nadu.

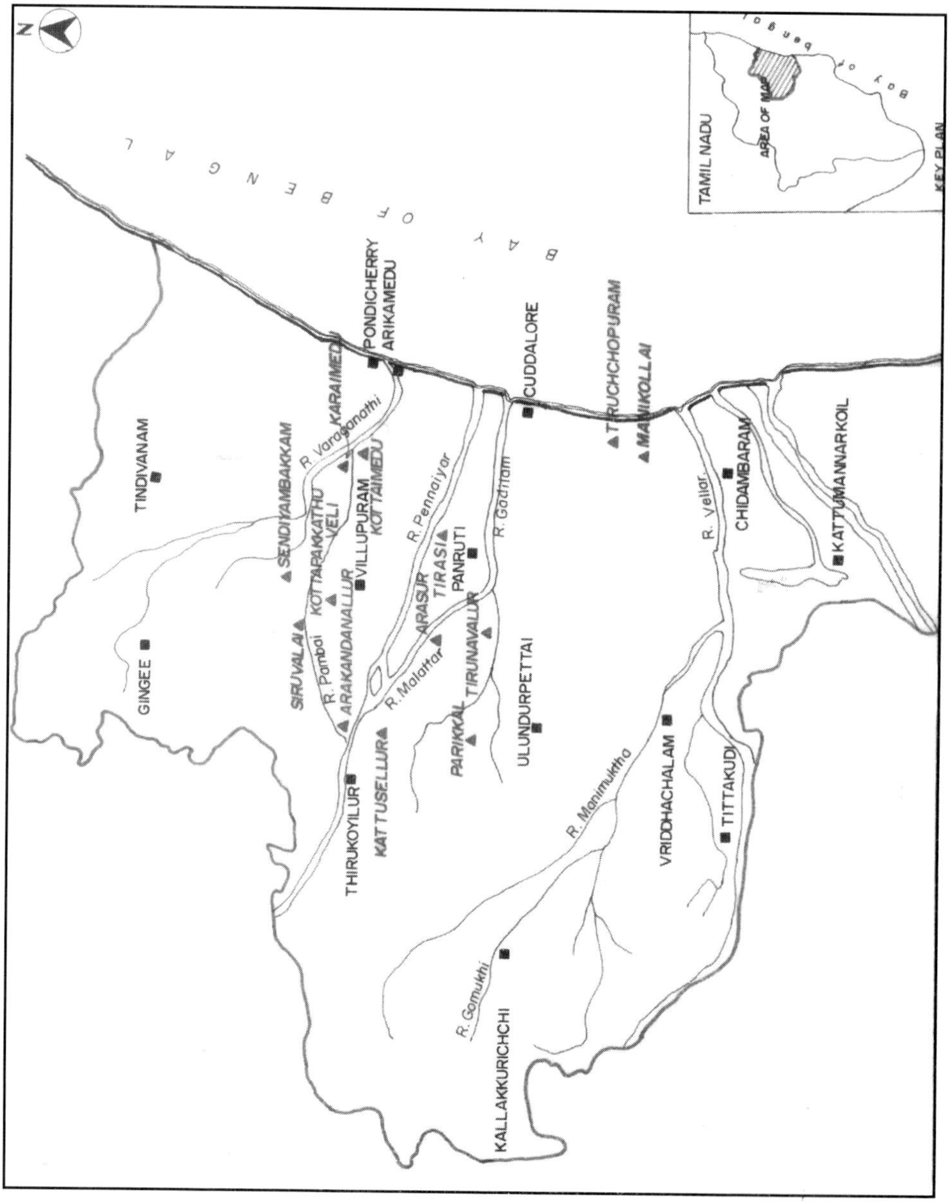

Fig. 06 :
Map showing recently discovered satellite settlements of Arikamedu.

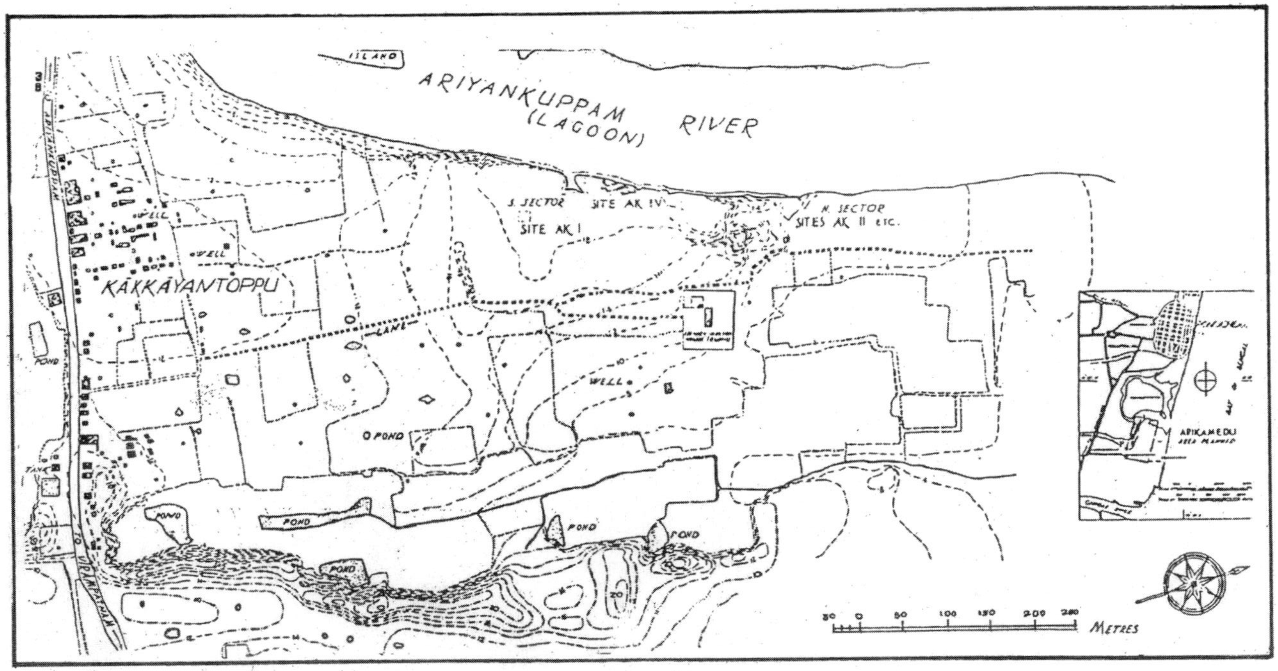

Fig. 07 : Site Plan of Arikamedu with contour (Wheeler et al., 1946).

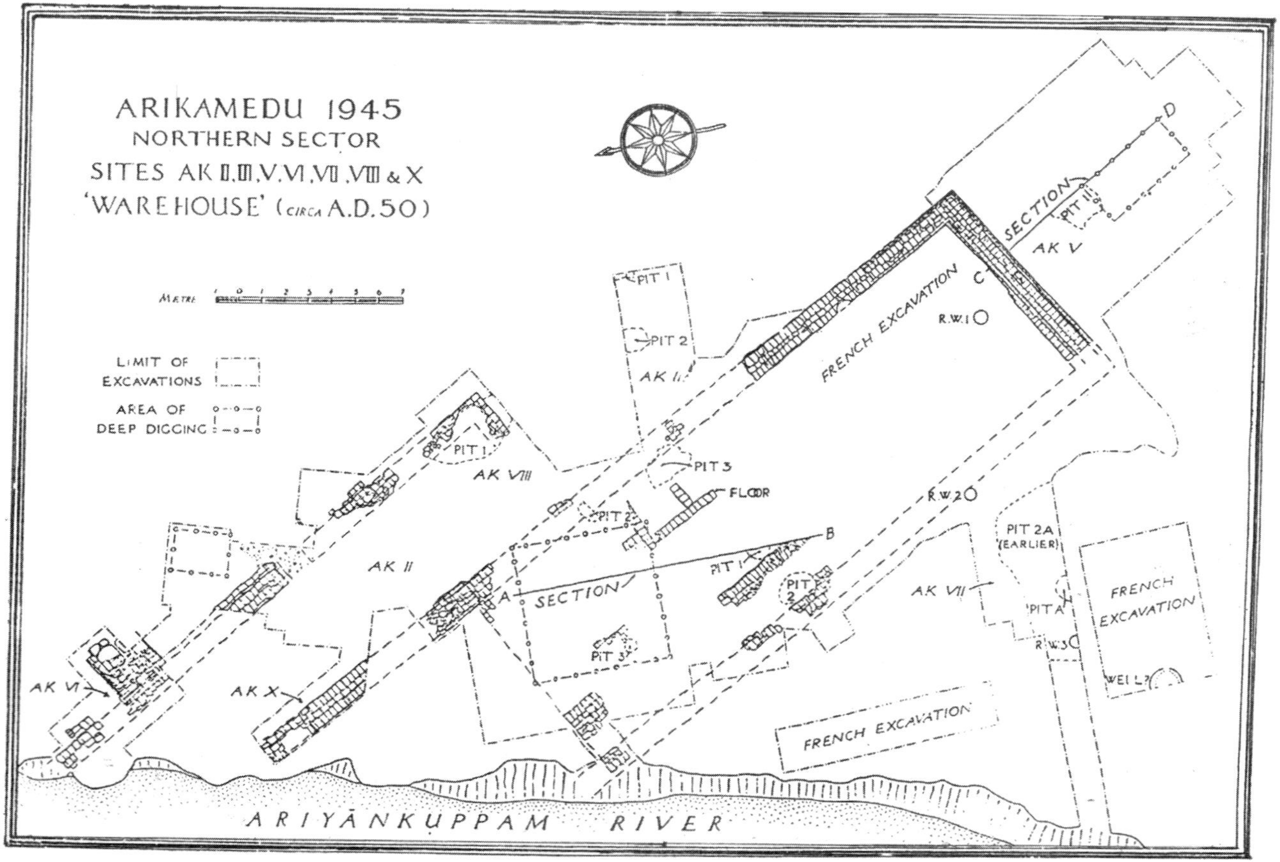

Fig. 08 : Arikamedu- Plan of Ware House in Northern Sector (Wheeler et al., 1946).

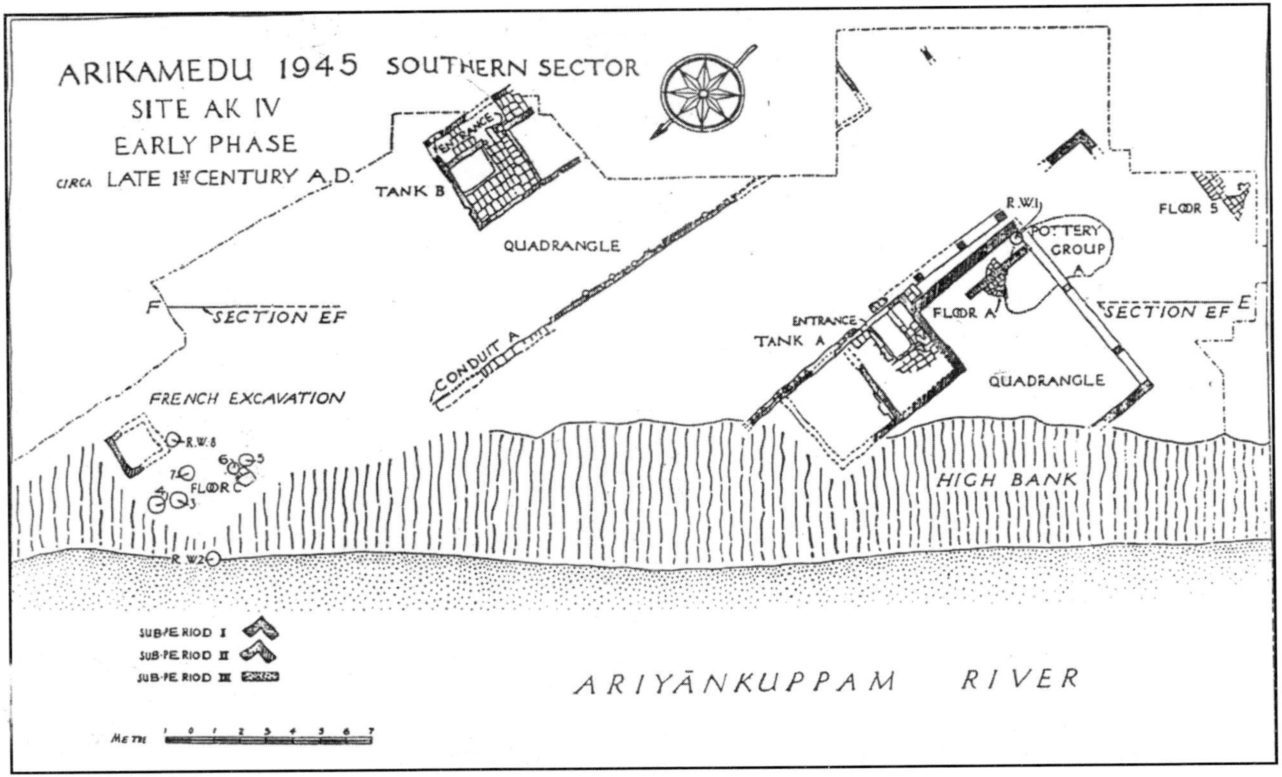

Fig. 09 : Plan of structures of early phase in southern sector (after Wheeler et al).

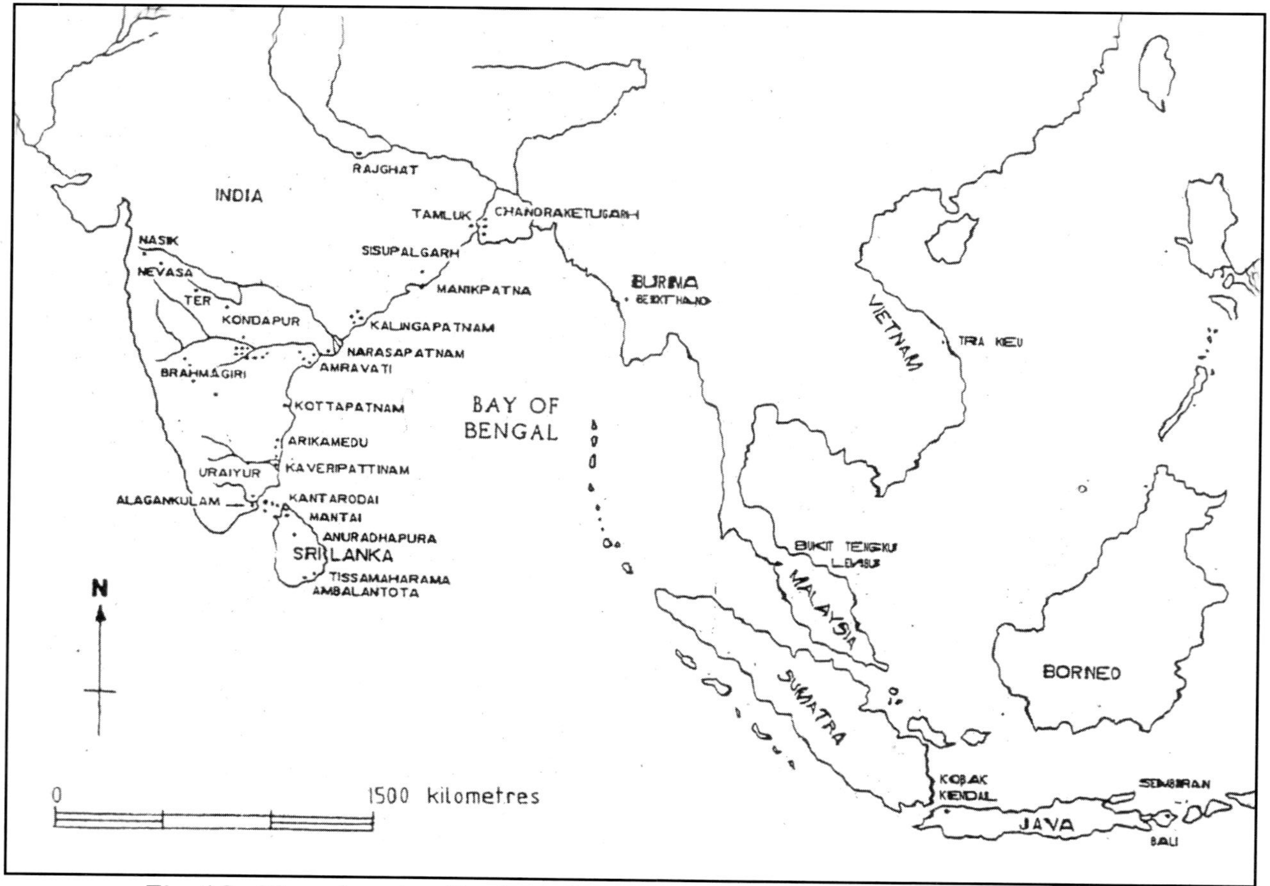

Fig. 10 : Map showing Rouletted ware sites in India and South East Asia.

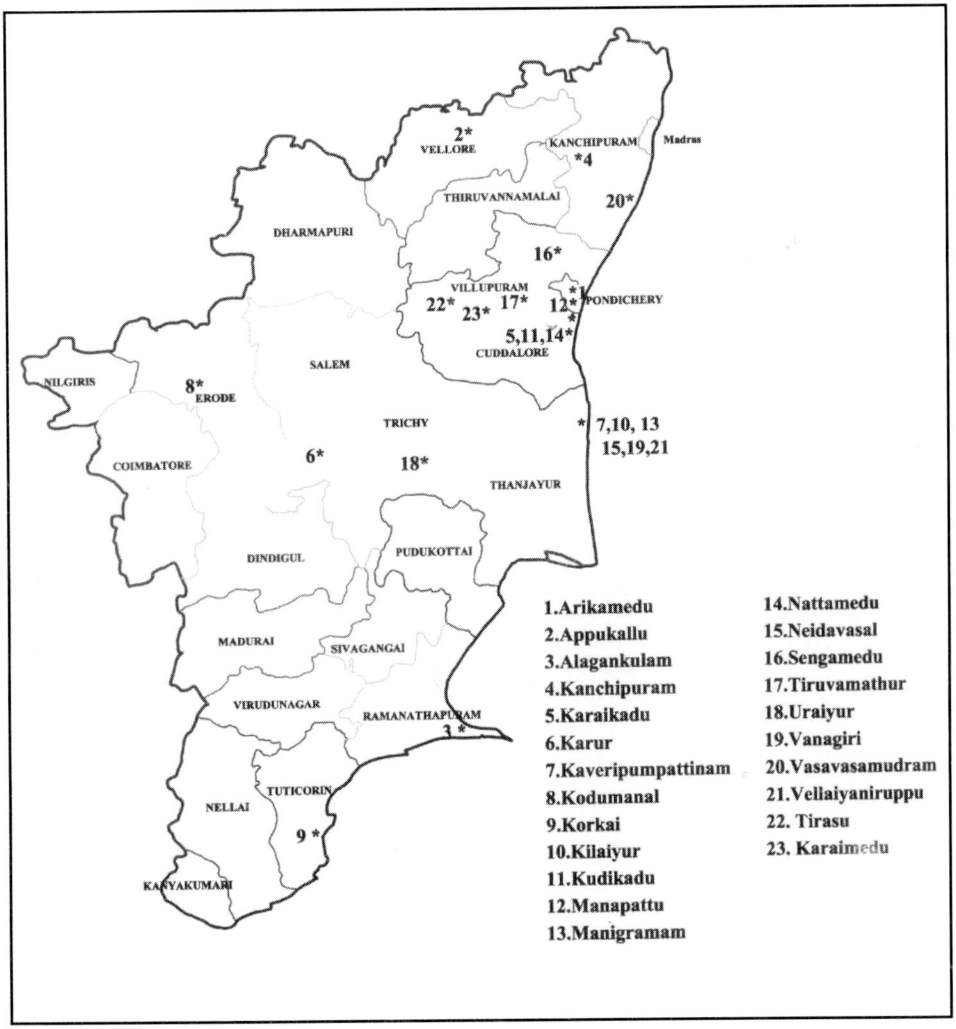

Fig. 11 : Rouletted ware sites in Tamil Nadu.

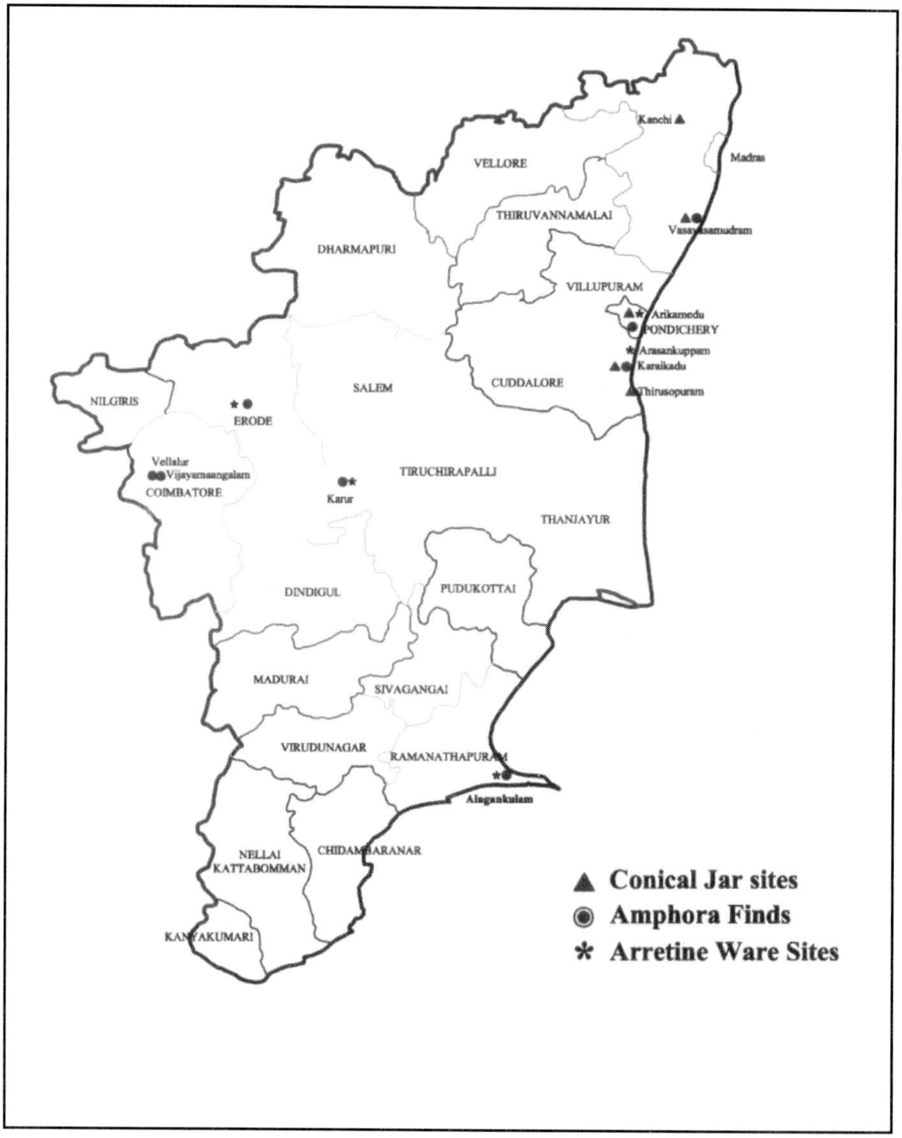

Fig. 12 : Arretine ware, Amphora and Conical jar sites in Tamil Nadu.

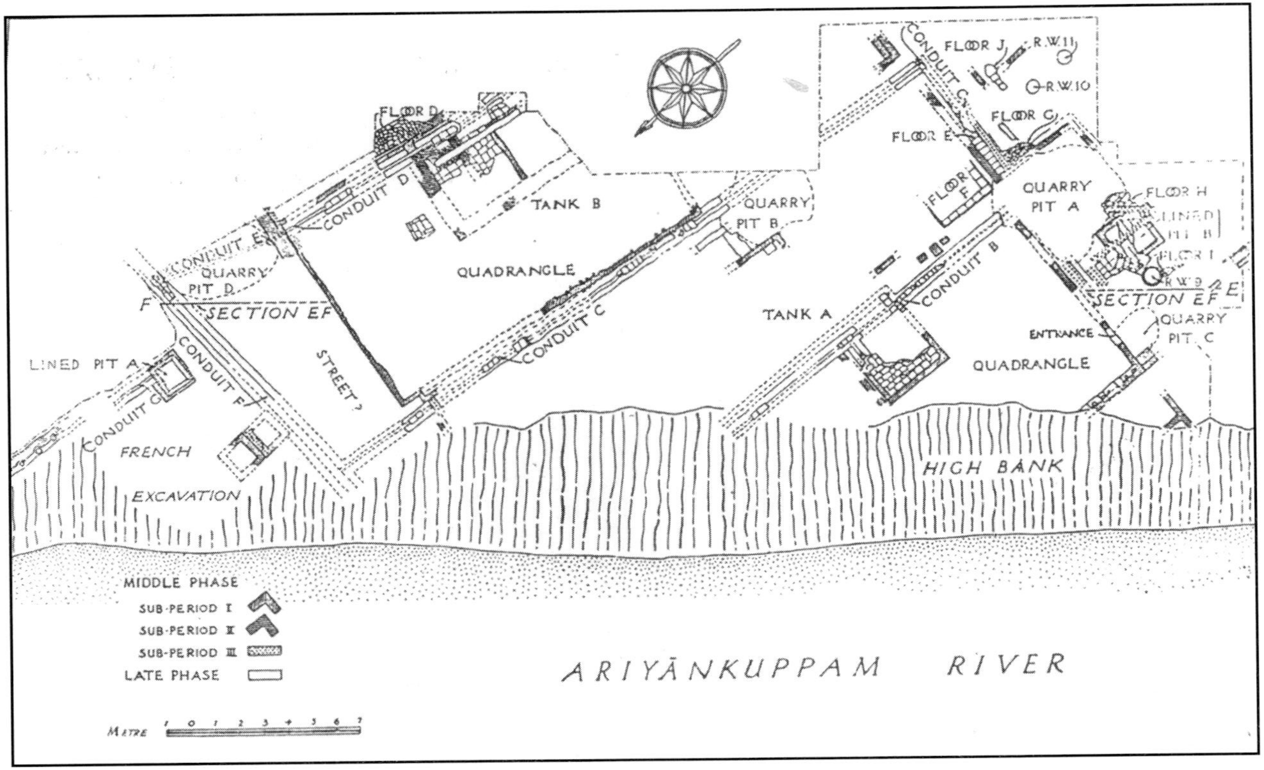

Fig. 13 : Layout of structures belonging to the Middle and Late phases of occupation at Arikamedu and submergence of the settlement (after Wheeler et al).

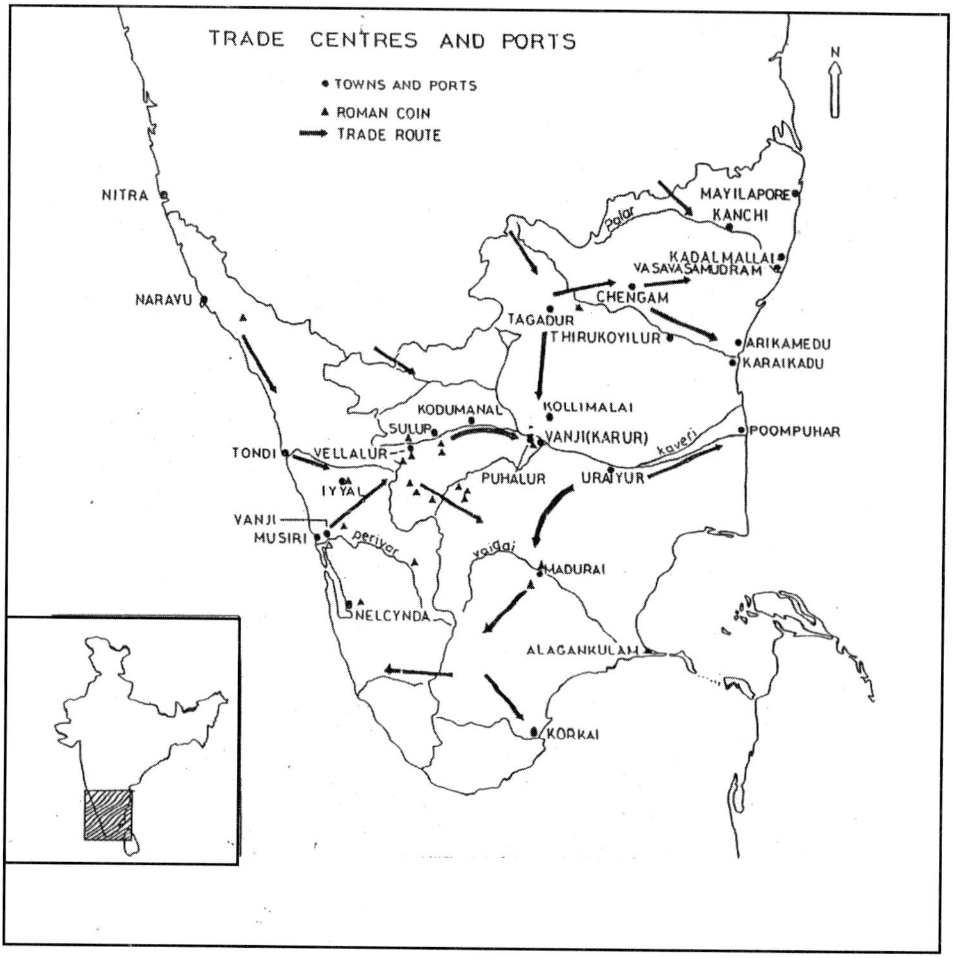

Fig. 14 : Map showing Trade centers and Ports in Tamil Nadu.

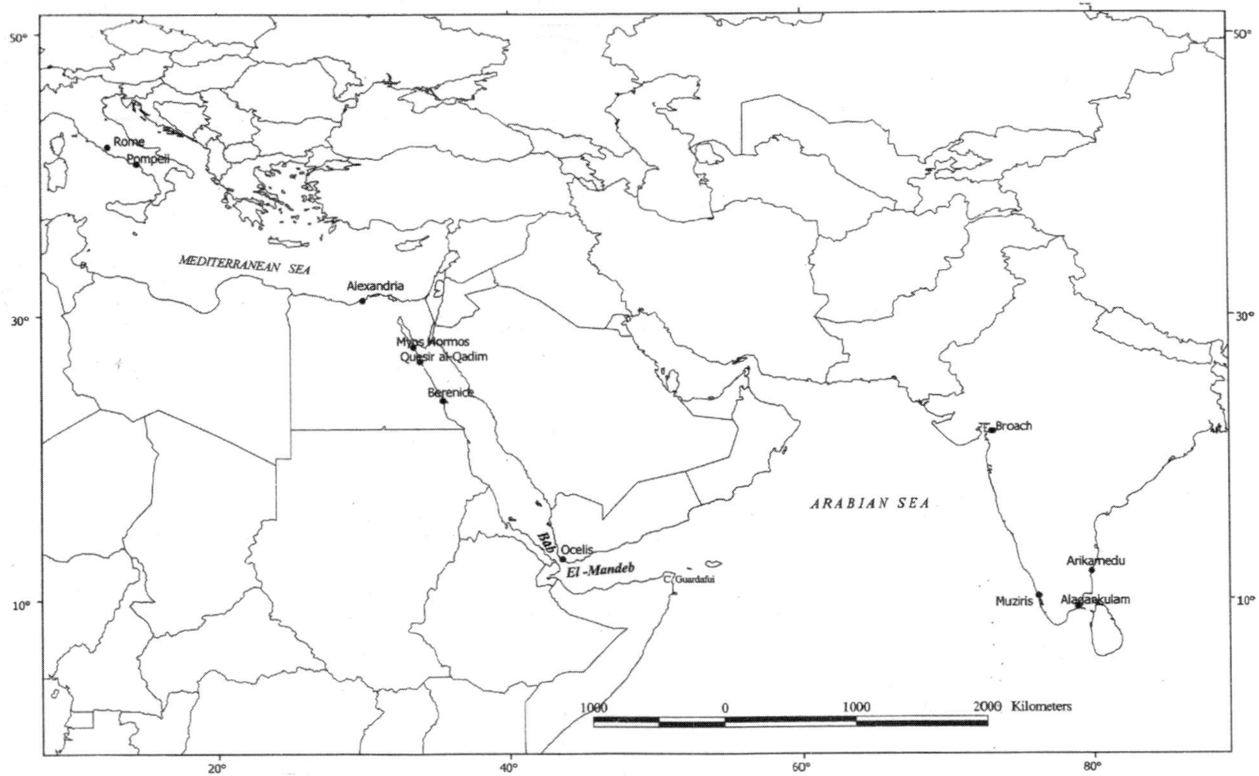

Fig. 15 : Map showing important sites on the ancient trade routes between Rome and India.

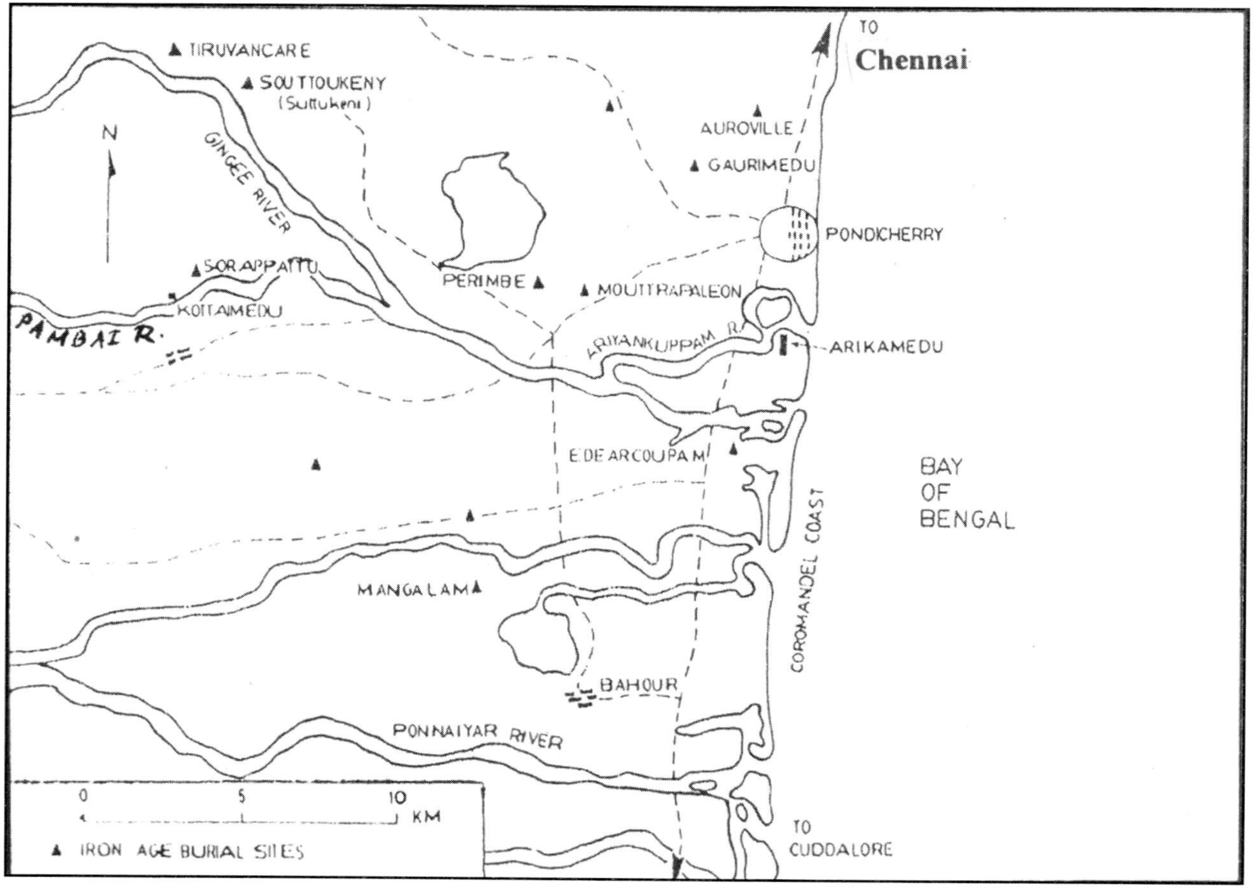

Fig. 16 : Map showing Arikamedu and late iron Age burial sites in the vicinity of Pondicherry.

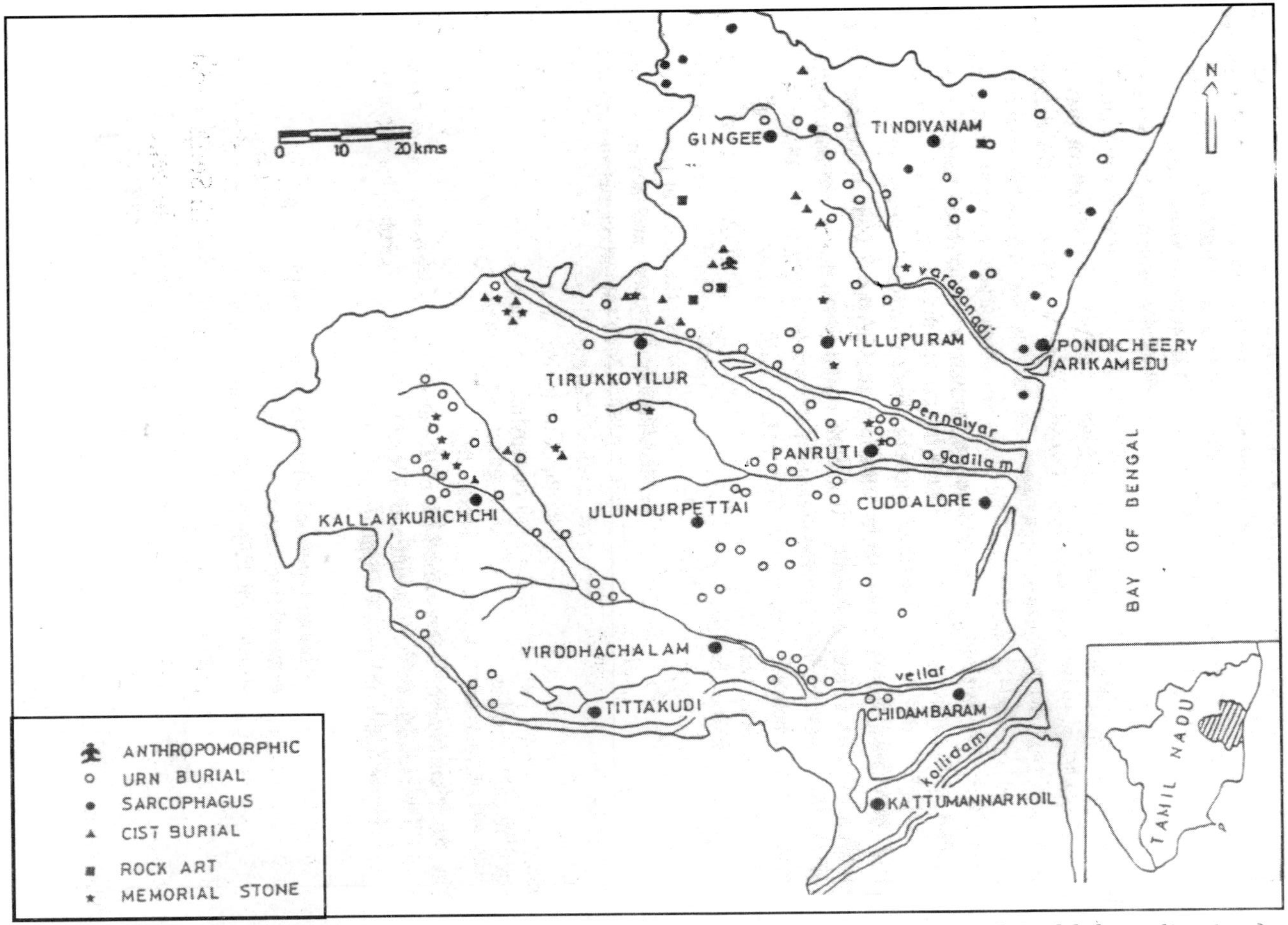

Fig. 17 : Megalithic sites in old South Arcot region (i.e. present Villupuram and Cuddalore districts).

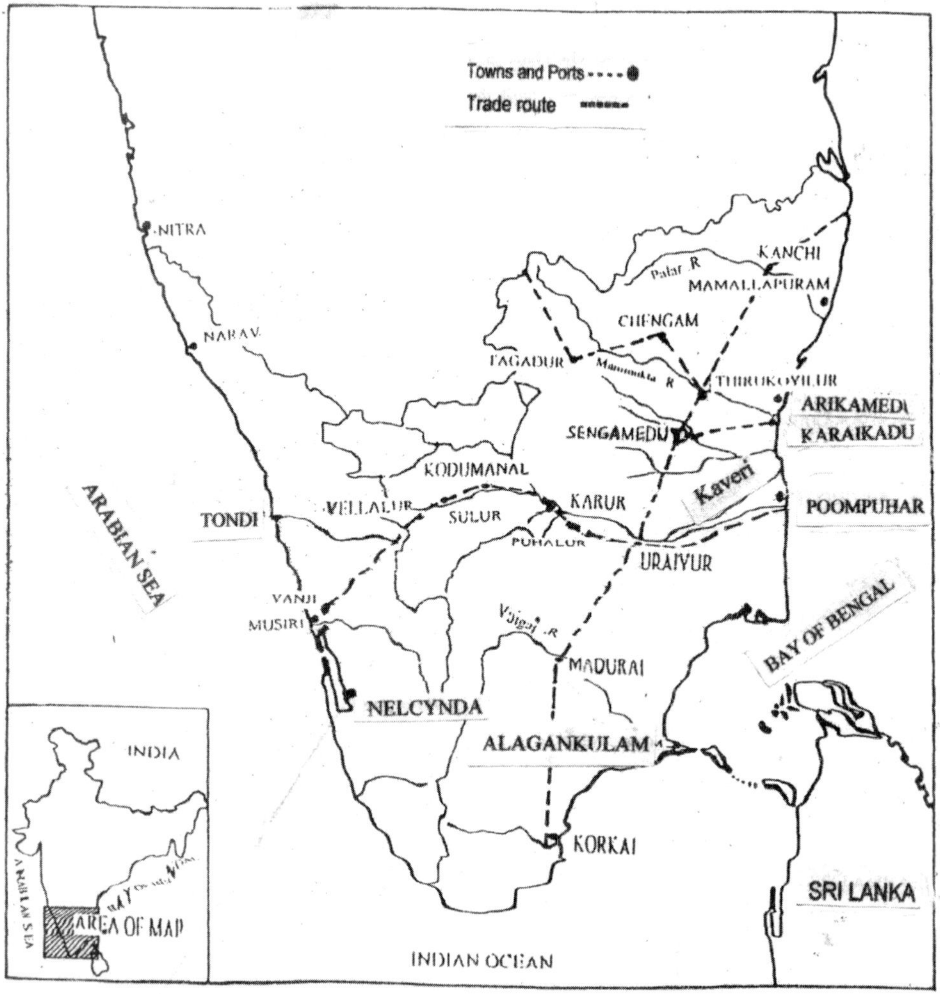

Fig. 18 : Map showing Arikamedu's Trade contacts with Sengamedu and other important Satellite settlements and Trade centers.

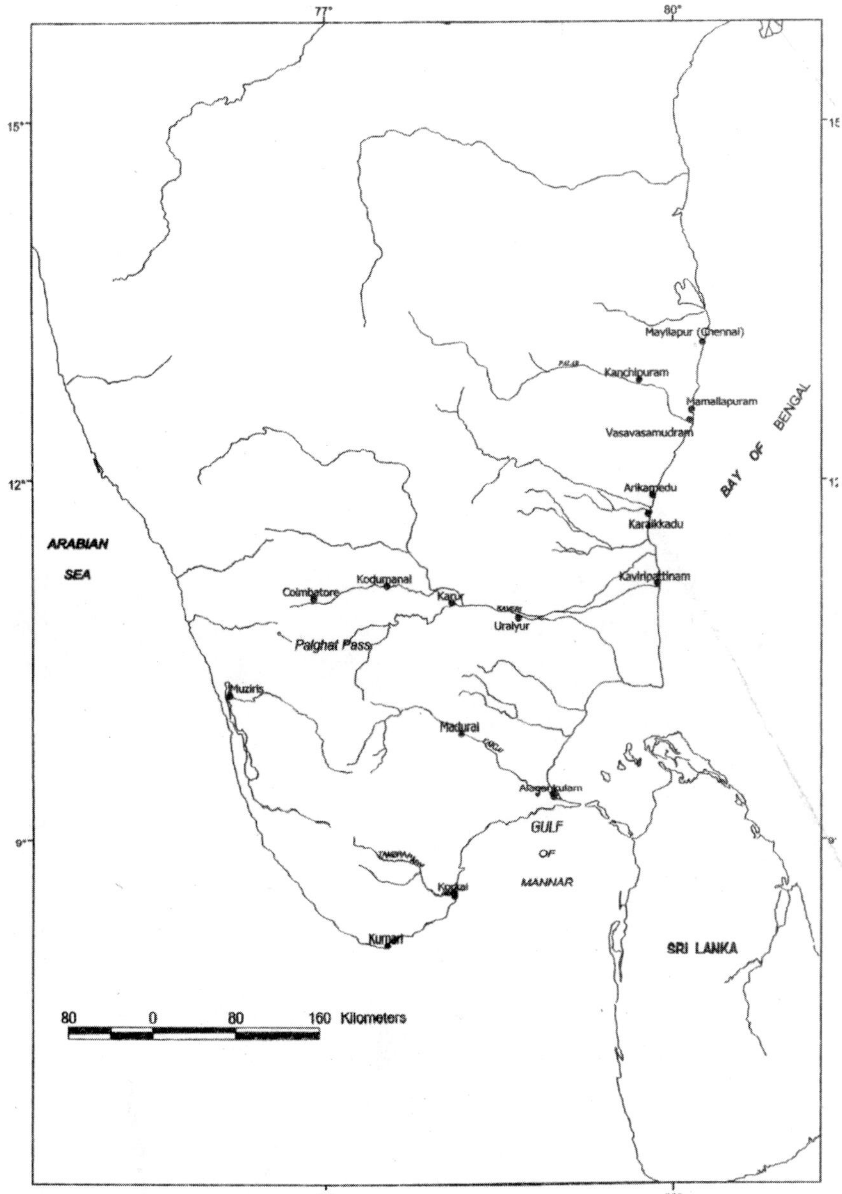

Fig. 19 : Map showing important sites connected with the Roman trade in South India.

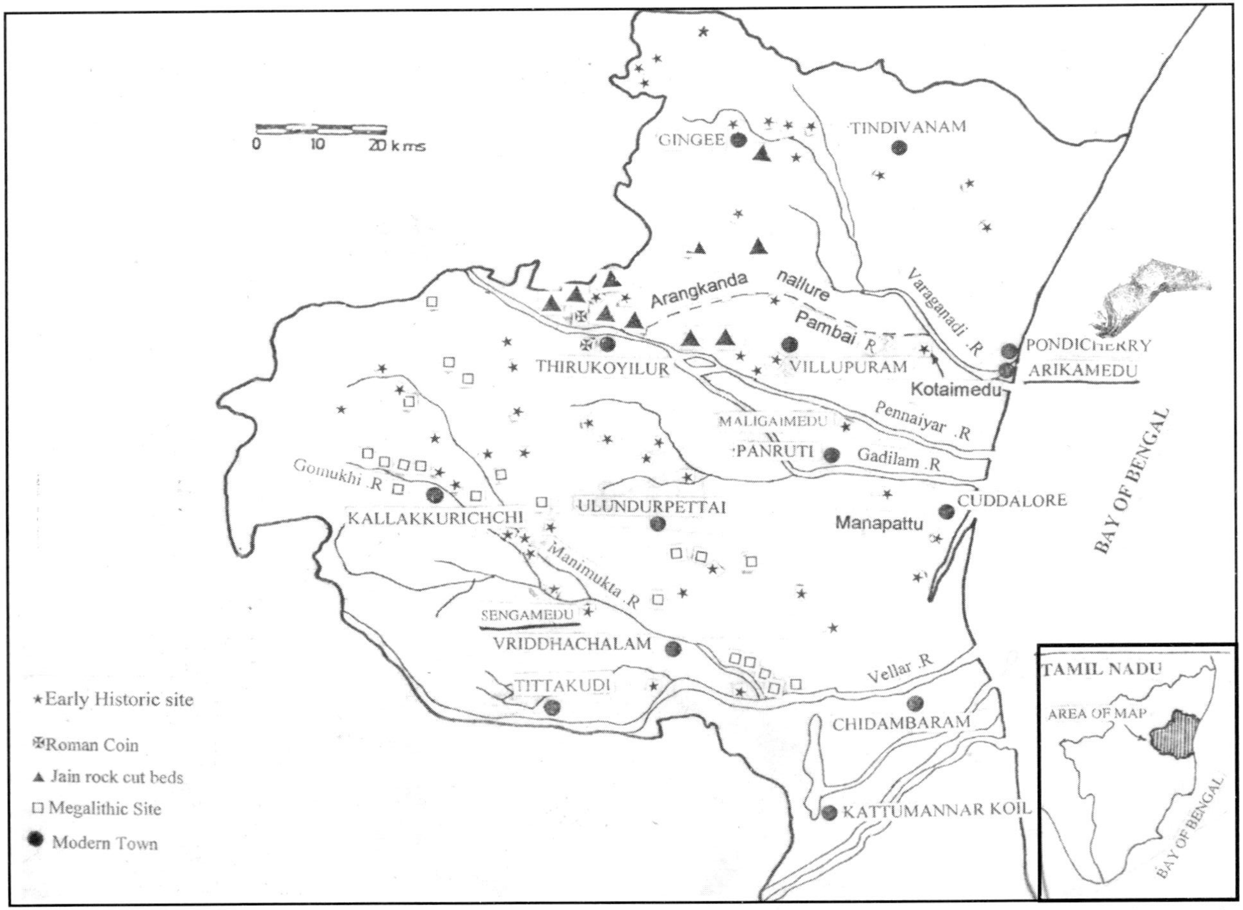

Fig. 20 : Early Historic phase in old South Arcot region (i.e. present Villupuram and Cuddalore districts).

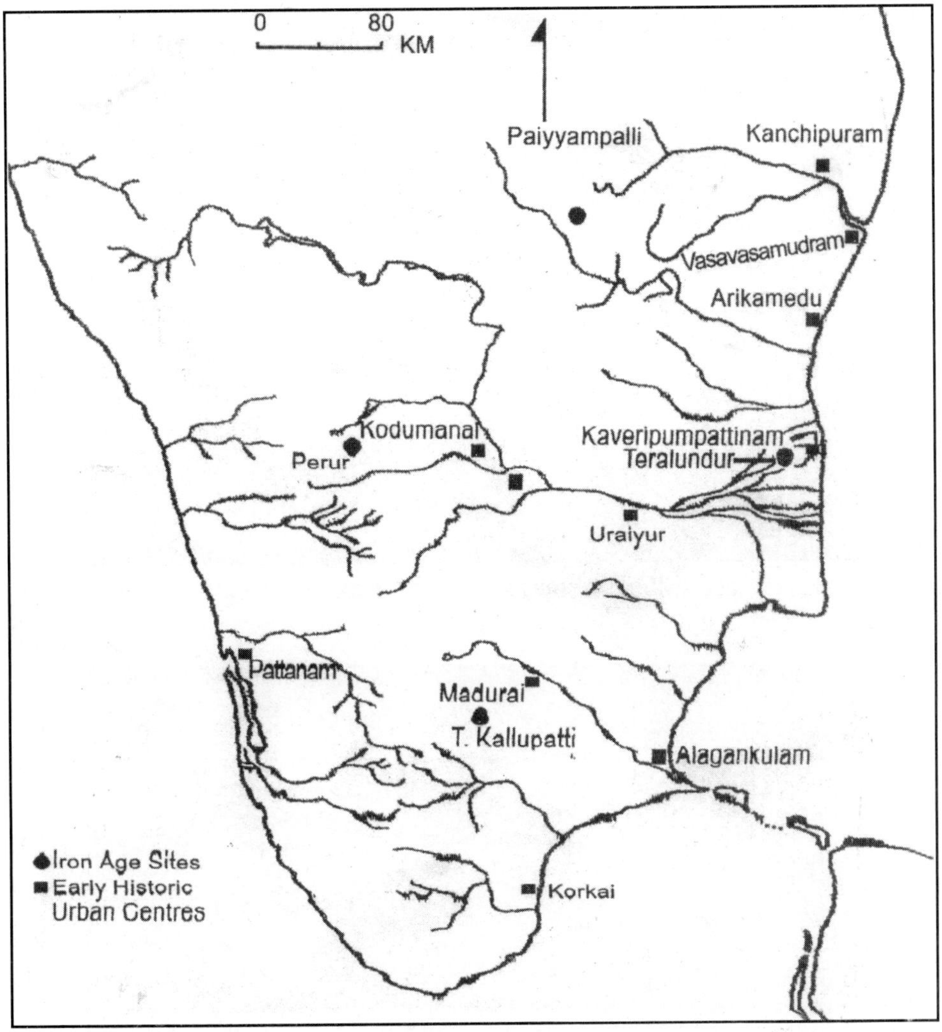

Fig. 21 : Iron Age and Early Historic sites of South India.

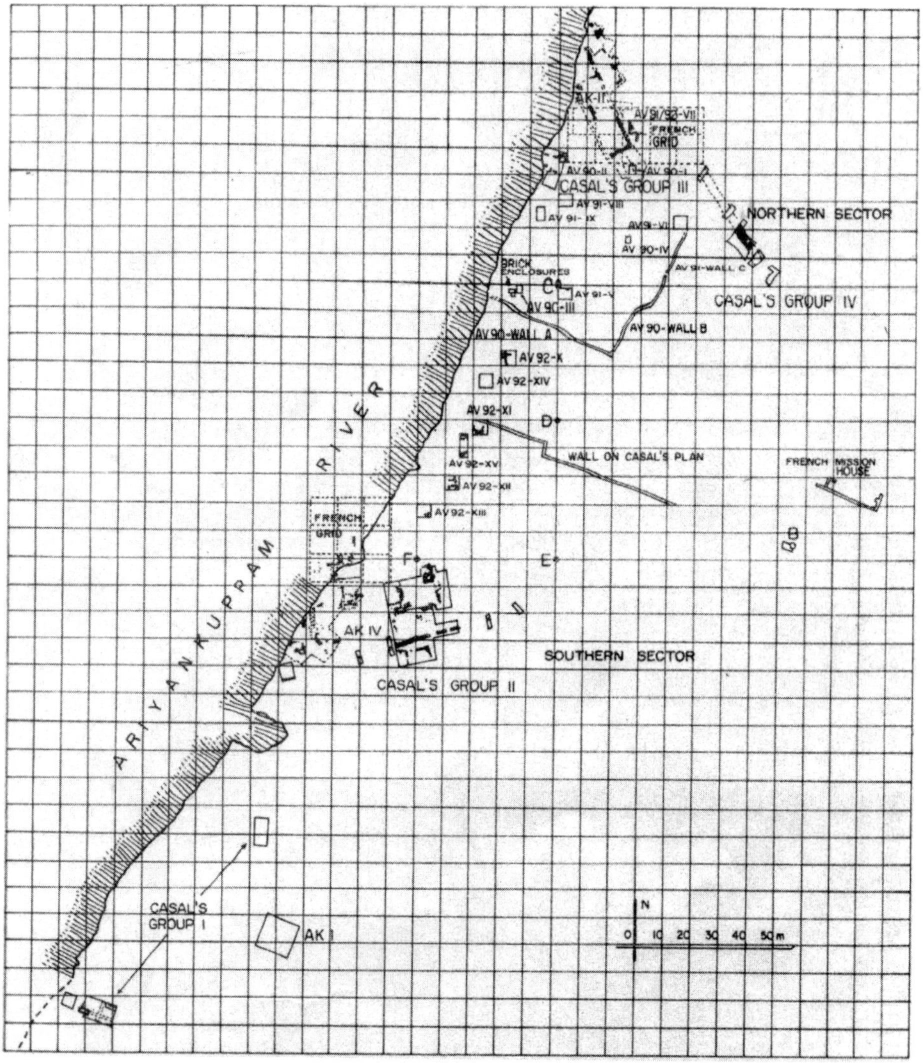

Fig. 22 : Plan of Arikamedu prepared by V. Begley (1992).

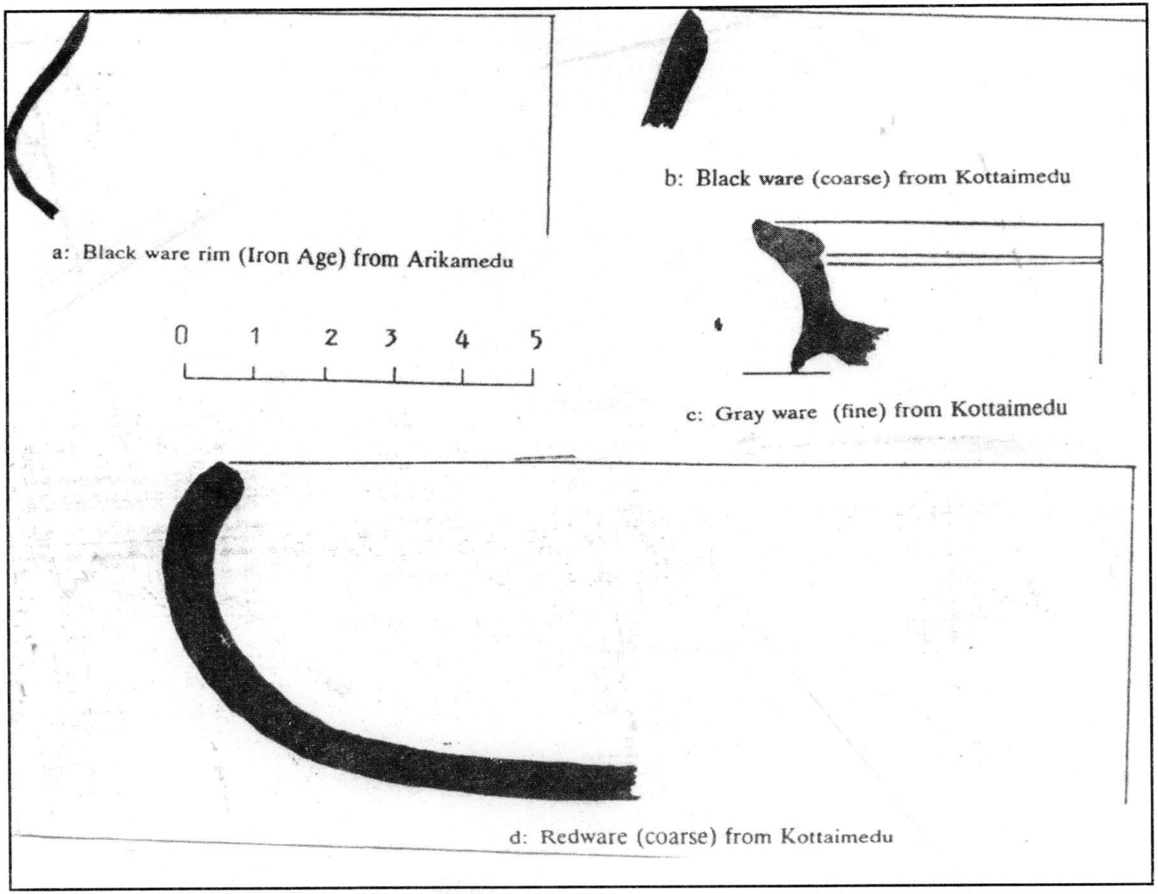

Fig. 23 : Pottery Reconstruction, from Arikamedu and Kottaimedu.

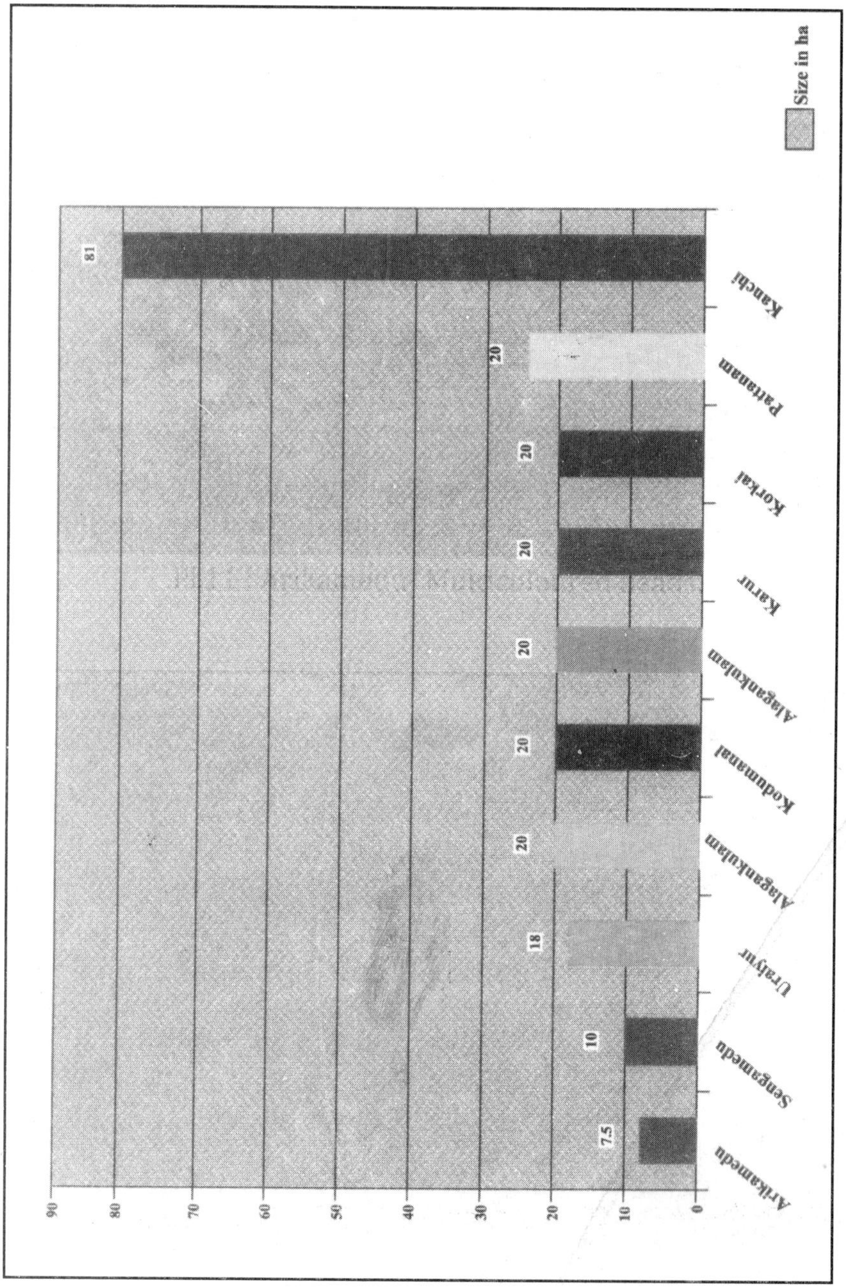

Fig. 24 : Size of Urban centers in Tamil country.

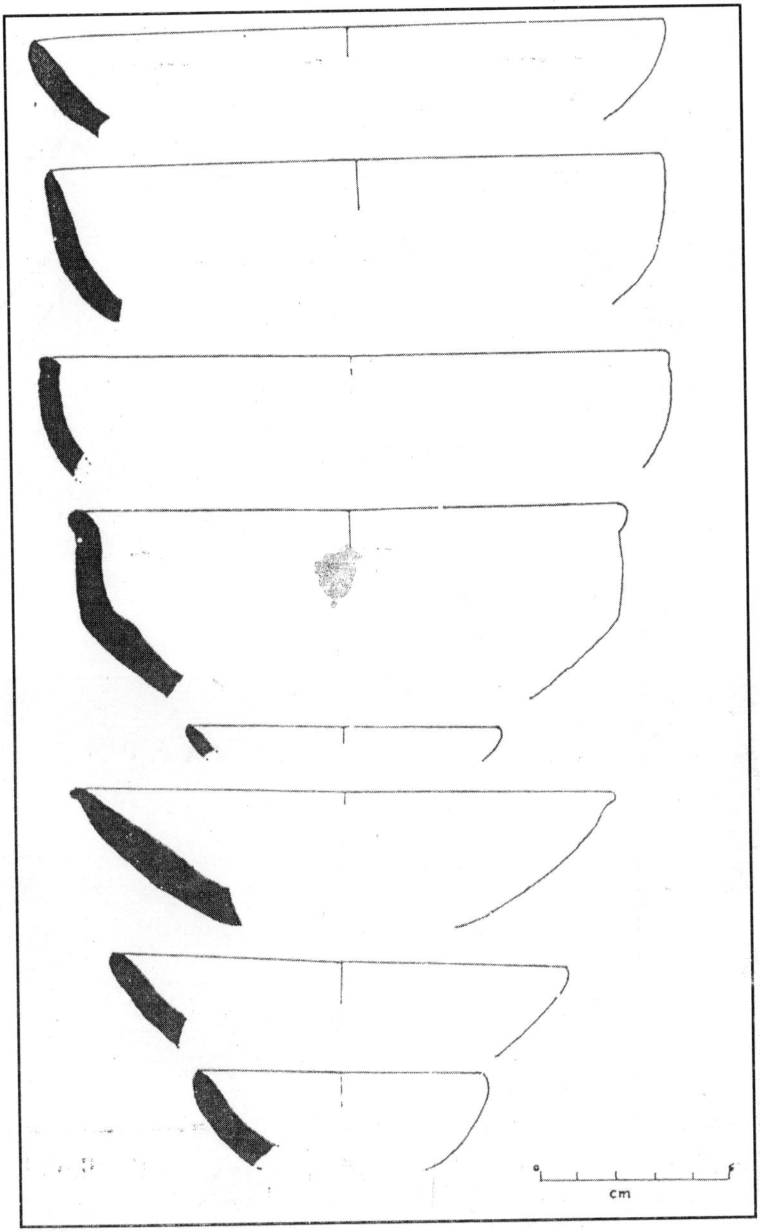

Fig. 25 : Line drawing of Black and Red ware from Parikal.

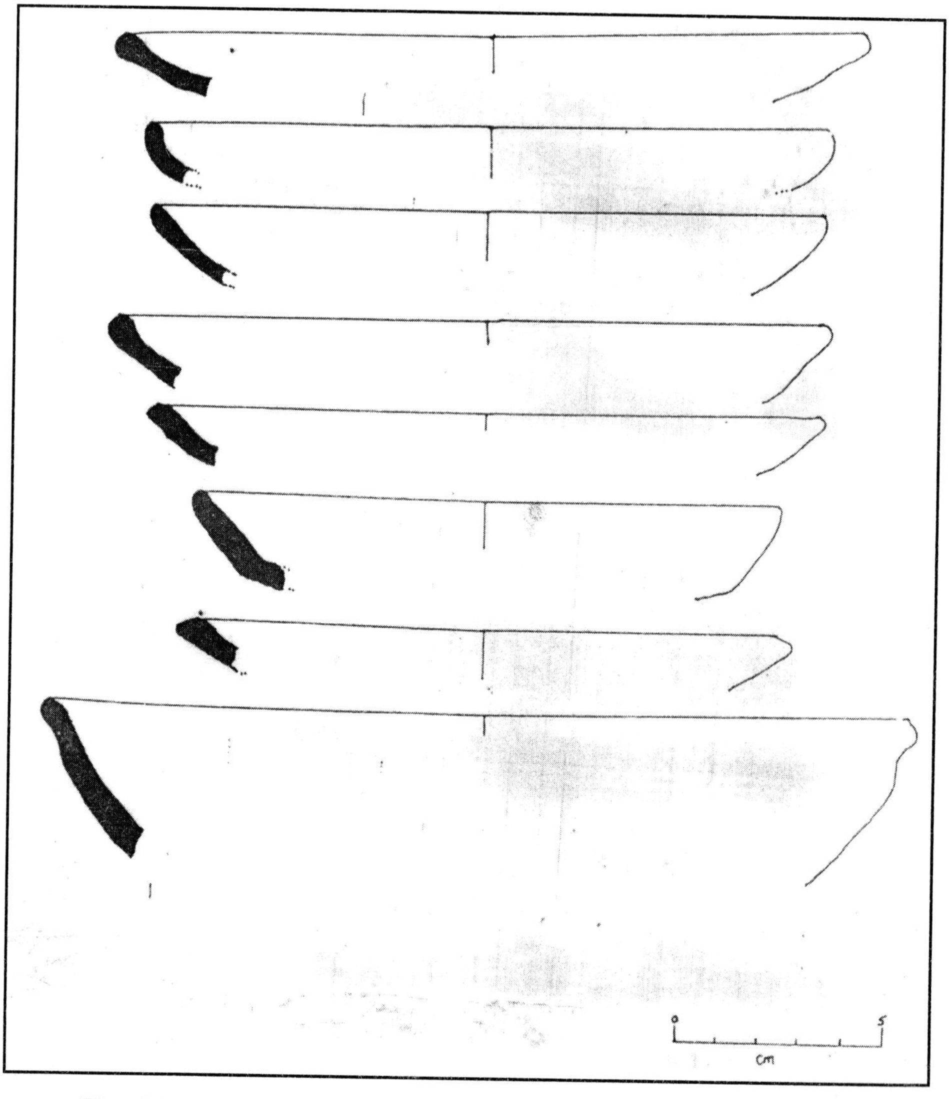

Fig. 26 : Line drawing of Coarse Red ware from Manikolai.

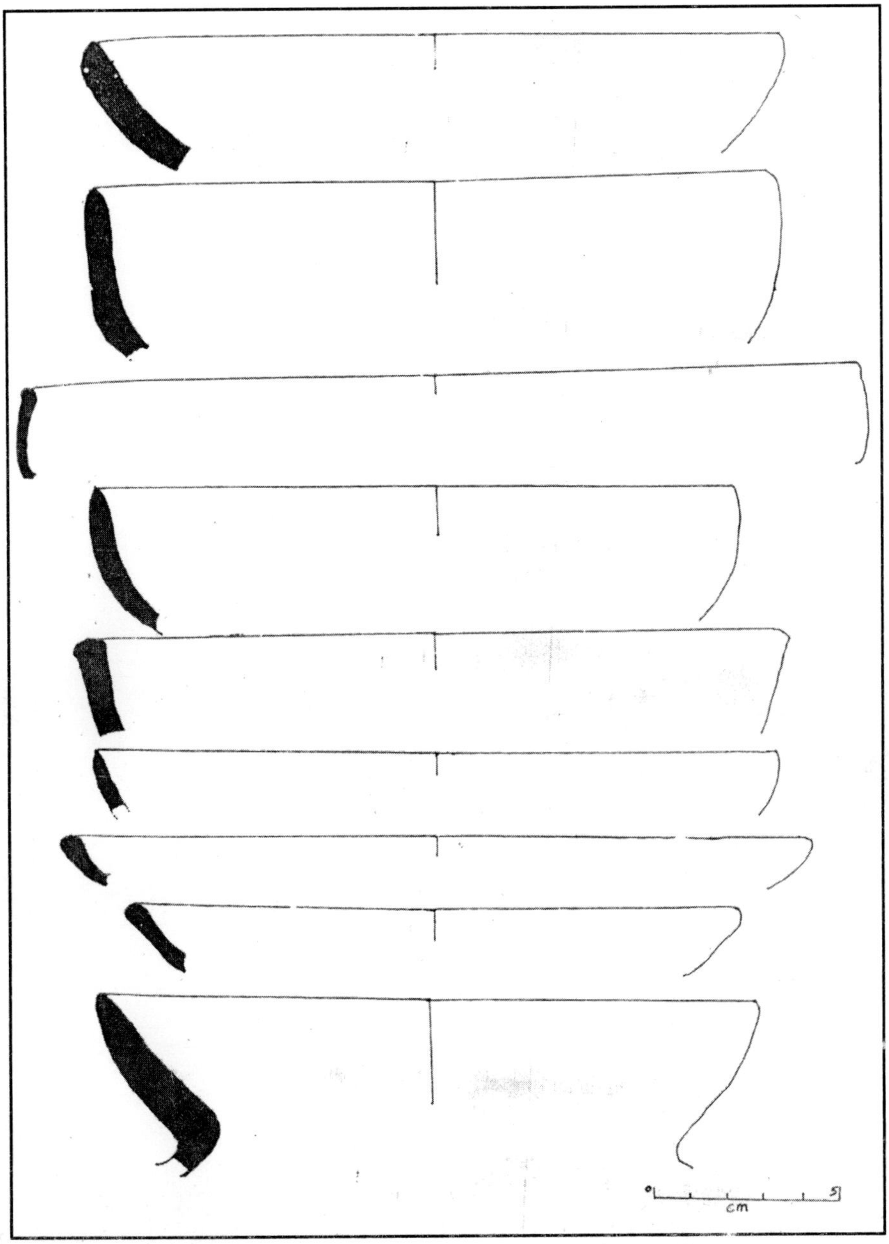

Fig. 27 : Line drawing of Coarse Red ware from Thirusopuram.

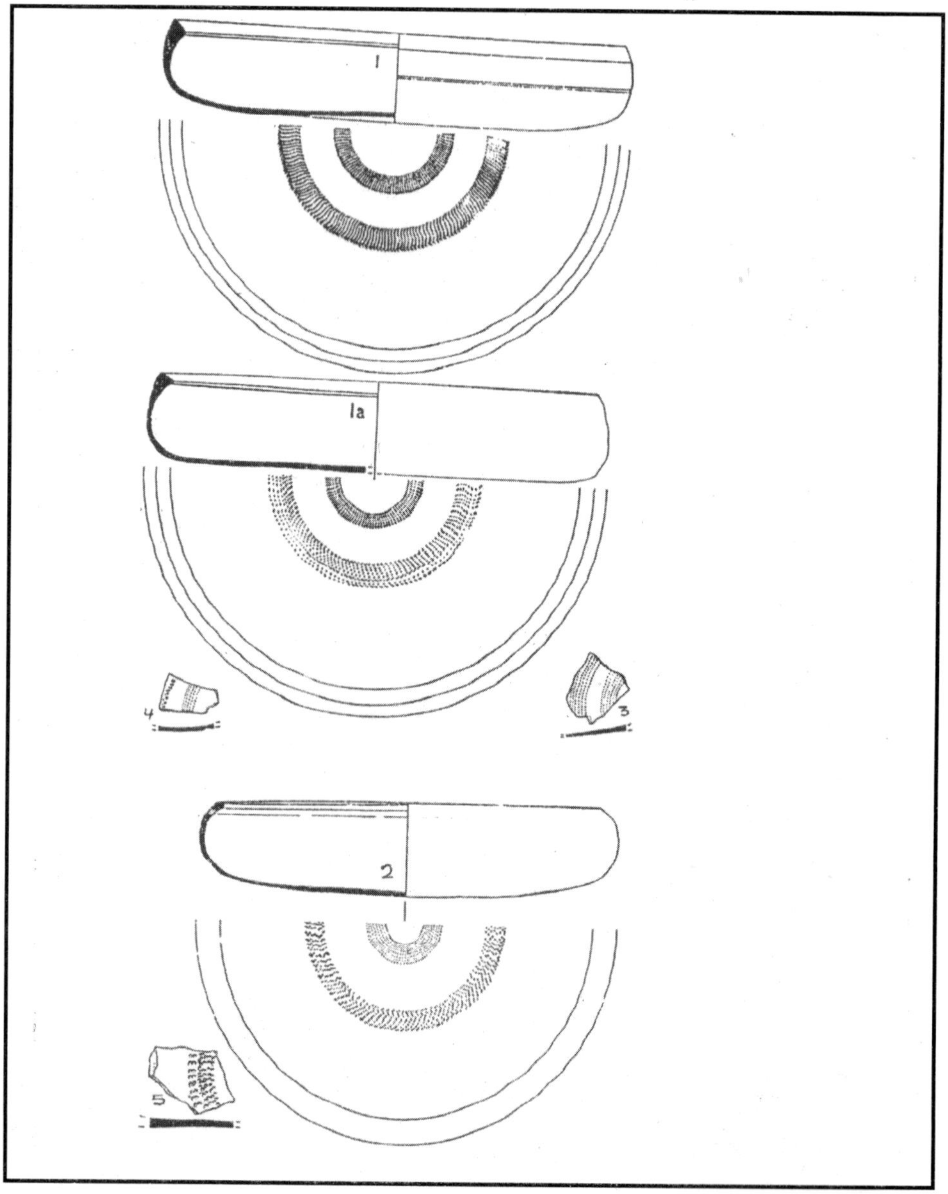

Fig.28 : Rouletted ware from 1 & 1a Arikamedu, 2 Brahmagiri, 3-5 Satanikota.

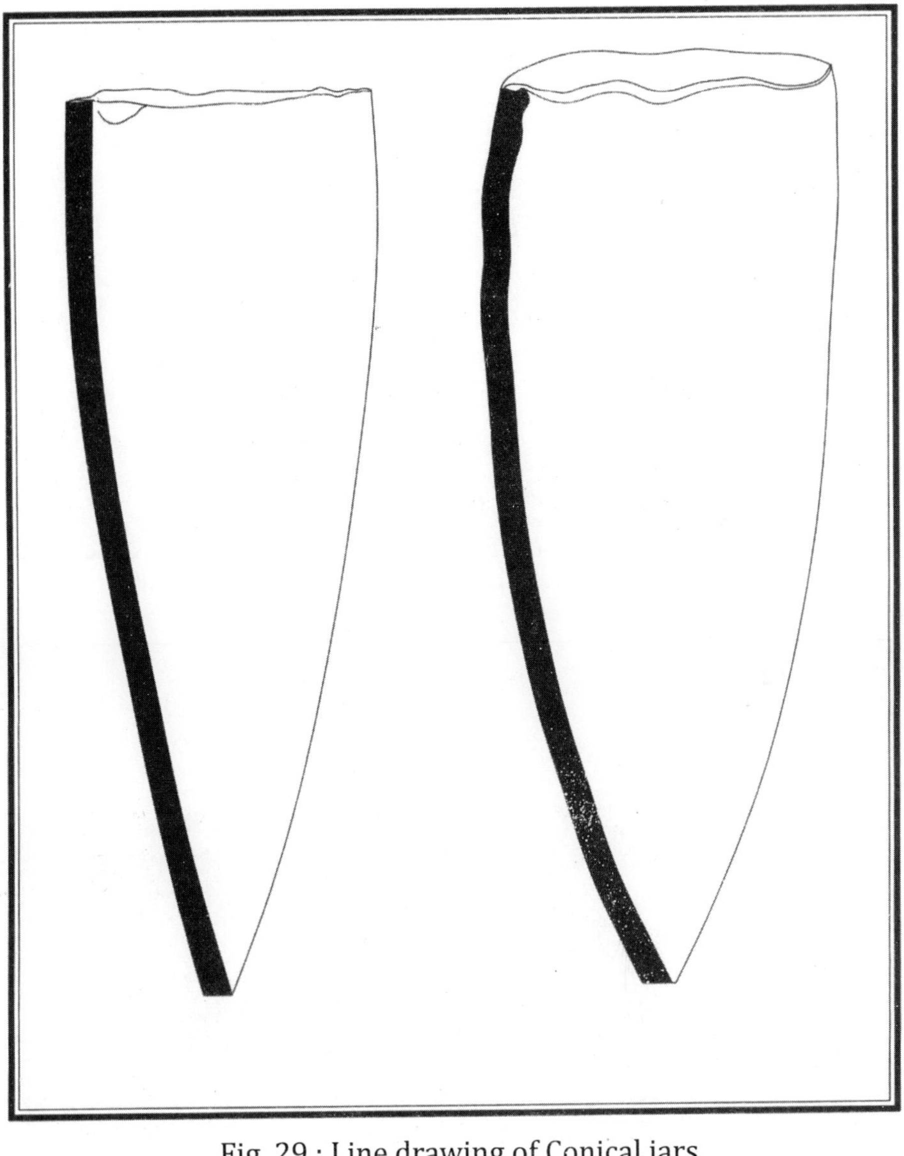

Fig. 29 : Line drawing of Conical jars.

PLATES

Pl.1 : Arikamedu – General view at present.

Pl.2 : Arikamedu on the banks of river Ariyankuppamr.

Pl.3 : Arikamedu excavation in progress (Wheeler et al., 1946).

Pl.4 : Arikamedu – Brick enclosure (Wheeler et al., 1946).

Pl.5 : Arikamedu- South eastern wall of Ware House (Wheeler et al., 1946).

Pl.6 : Arikamedu- Ring Well (Wheeler et al., 1946).

Pl.7 : Arikamedu- Tank A (Wheeler et al., 1946).

Pl.8 : Arikamedu- Tank B (Wheeler et al., 1946).

Pl.9 : Arikamedu- Rouletted wares (Wheeler et al., 1946).

Pl.10 : Arikamedu- Inscribed potsherds (Wheeler et al., 1946).

Pl.11 : Arikamedu- Multicoloured beads.

Pl.12 : Arikamedu-Multicoloured beads and rough outs.

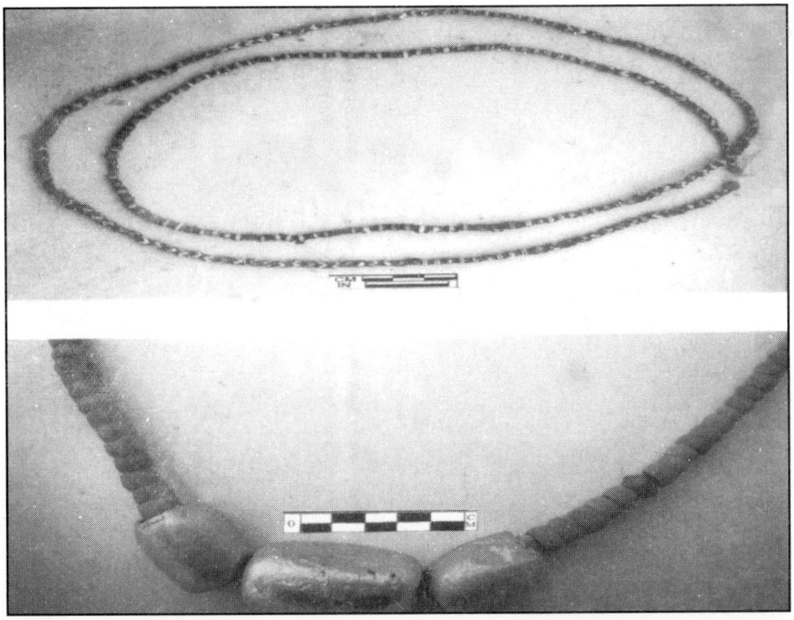

Pl.13 : Arikamedu- Glass bead Necklaces.

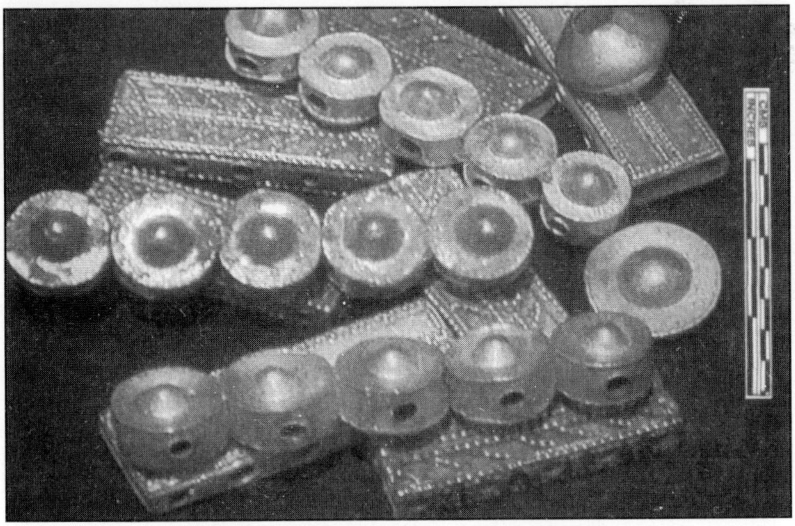

Pl.14 : Gold Strands – Suttukeni.

Pl.15 : Sengamedu – Ancient mound on the banks of the river Manikuktar.

Pl.16 : Sengamedu – Ruins of brick structure.

Pl.17 : Sengamedu – Ruins of bricks.

Pl.18 : Kottaimedu – Dry bed of river Pambai.

Pl.19 : Kottaimedu – Bricks used in ancient wall.

Pl.20 : Kottaimedu – Brick bats.

Pl.21 : Kottaimedu – Pottery with knob.

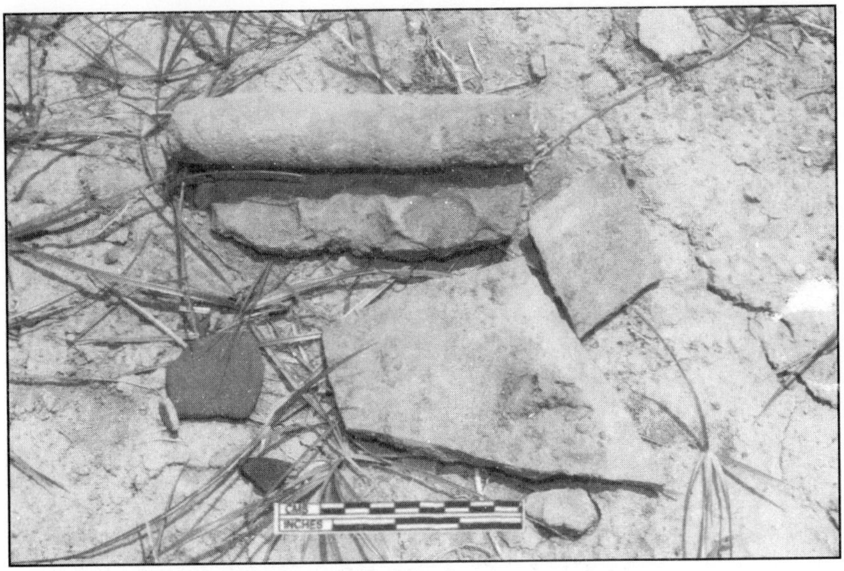

Pl.22 : Kottaimedu – Potsherds of Red Ware.

Pl.23 : Tirasu – General view.

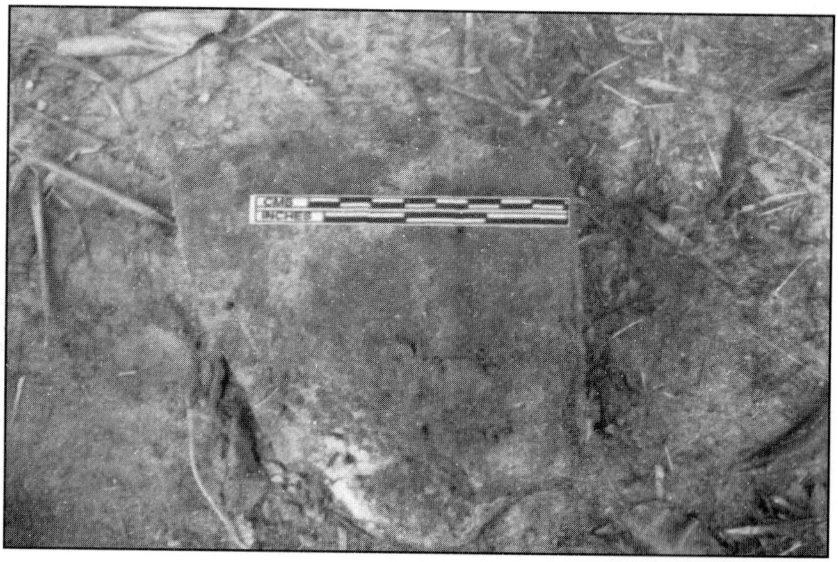

Pl.24: Tirasu – Broken ancient brick.

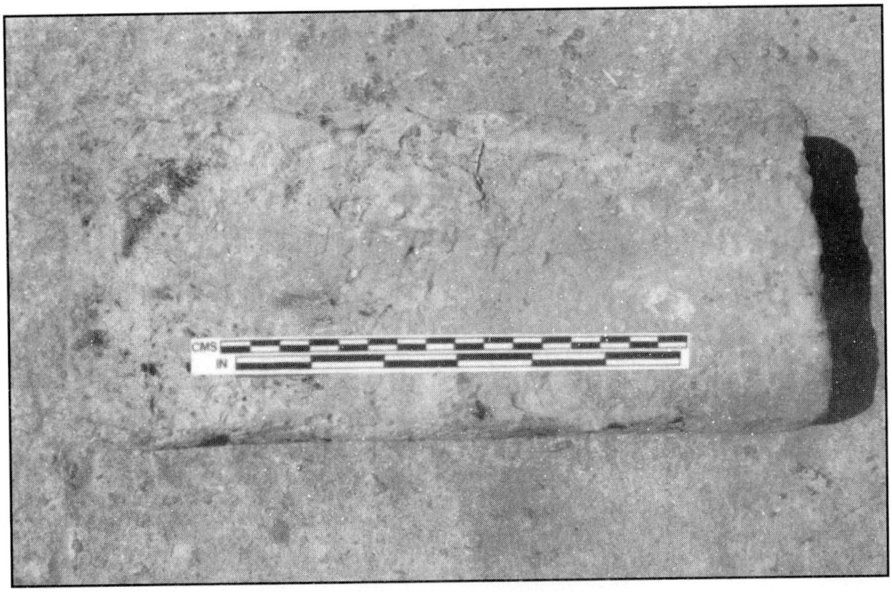

Pl.25 : Tirasu – Ancient brick.

Pl.26 : Karaimedu – Exposed section.

Pl.27 : Karaimedu – Broken urn.

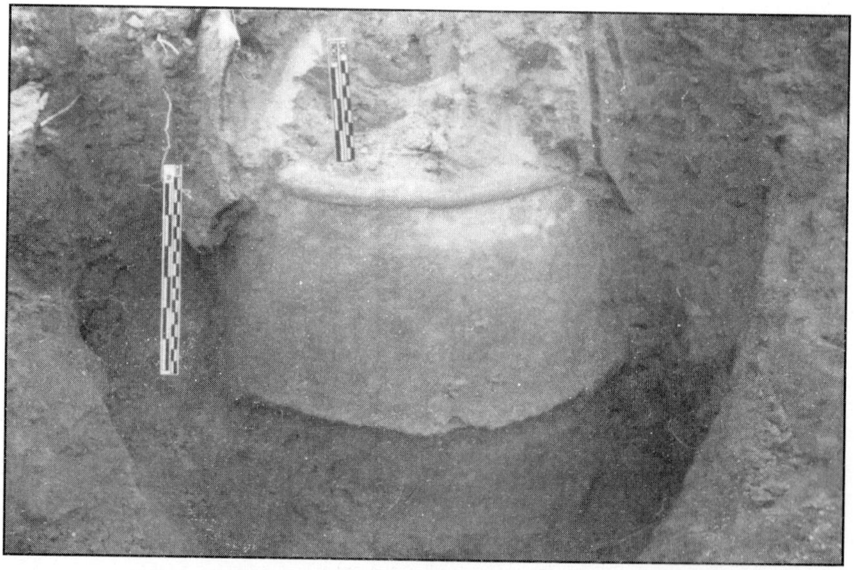

Pl.28 : Karaimedu – Ringwell shape urn burial.

Pl.29 : Karaimedu – Potsherds recovered from urn.

Pl.30 : River Pennar – near Arakandanallur.

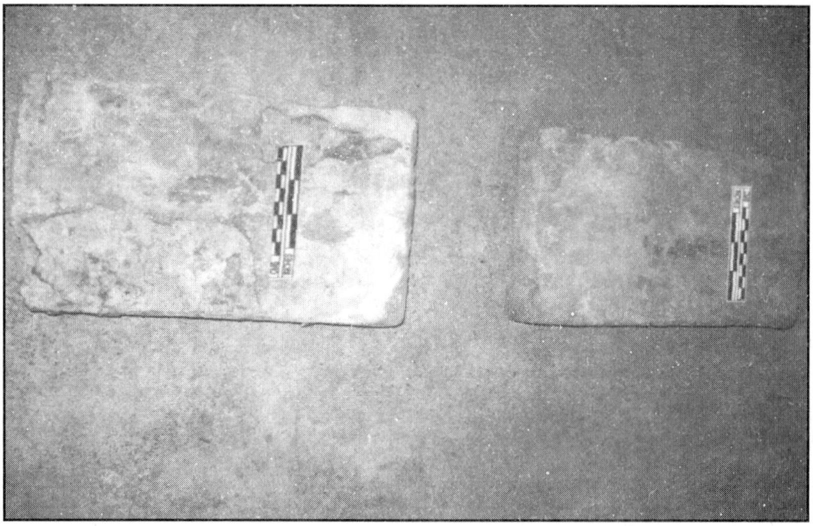

Pl.31 : Arakandanalur – Ancient bricks.

Pl.32 : Fragment of ancient brick found in river Pennar.

Pl.33 : Kottabakkatuveli – General view of the site.

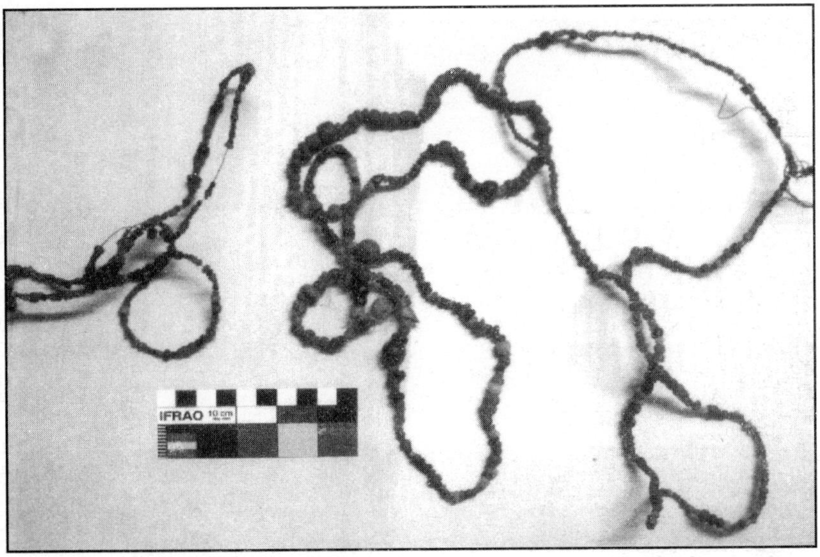

Pl.34 : Manikollai – Multicoloured glass beads.

Pl.35 : River Uppanar – near Thirusopuram.

Pl.36 : Thirusopuram – river section with potsherds.

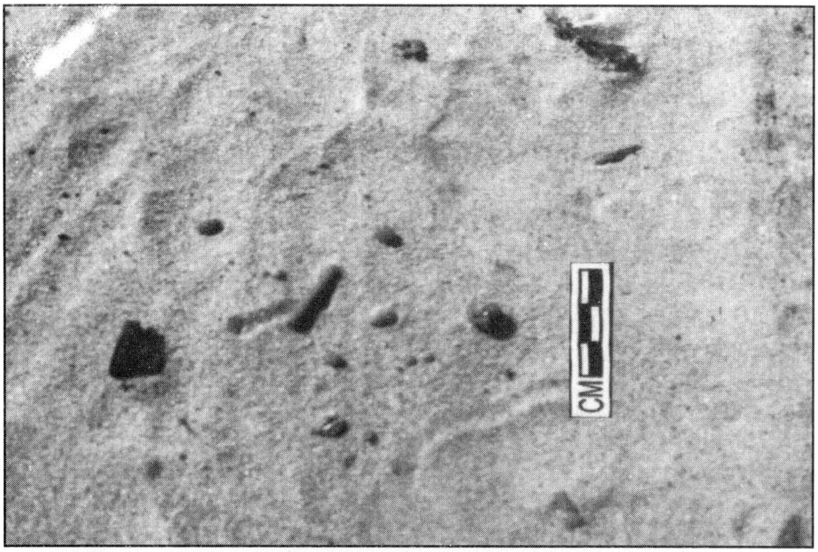

Pl.37 : Thirusopuram – Glass beads on the surface.

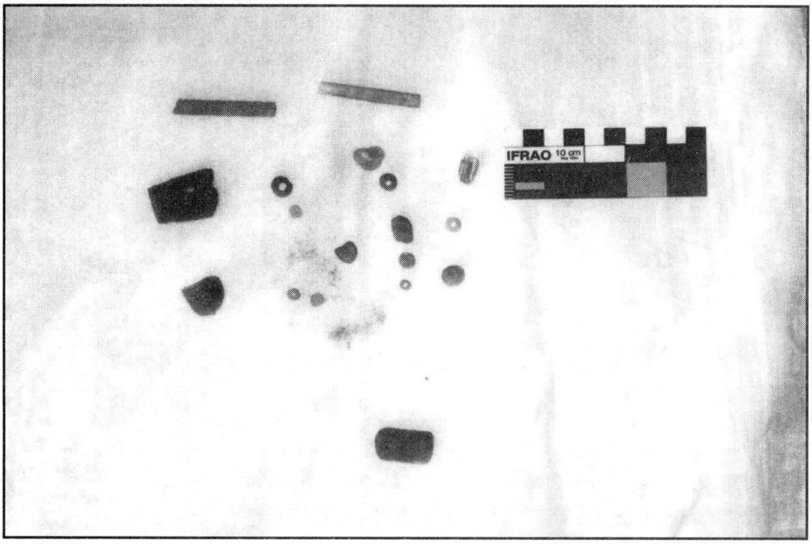

Pl.38 : Thirusopuram – Glass beads.

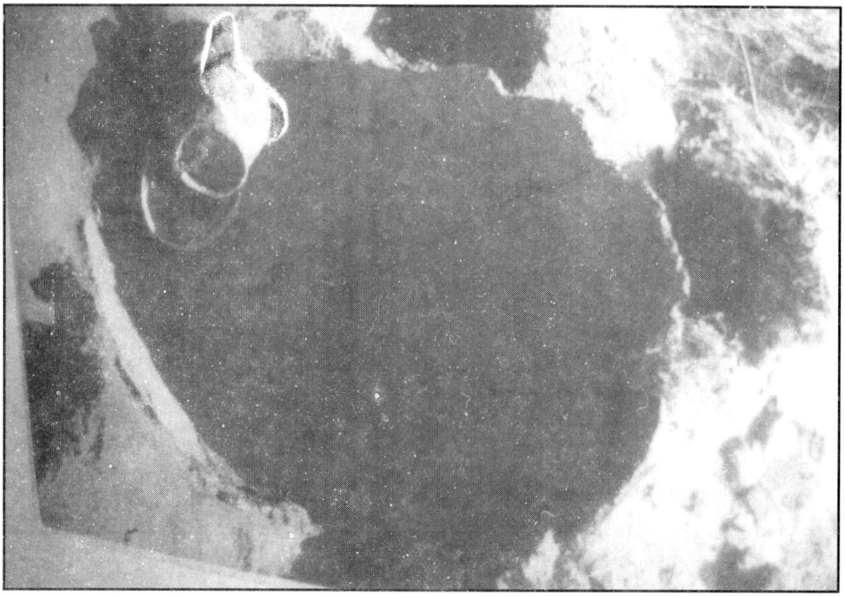

Pl.39 : Urn burial – Thiruvakkarai.

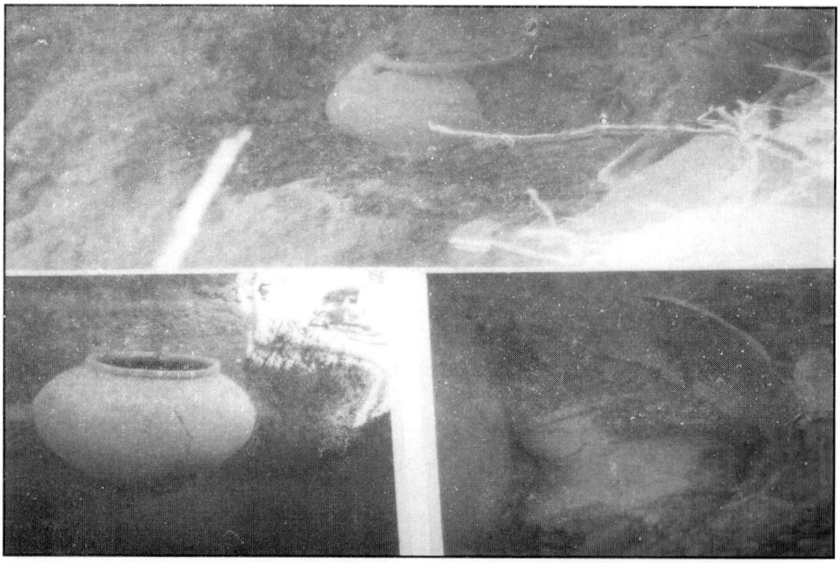

Pl.40 : Urn burials – Auroville.

Pl.41 : Region A – Cuddalore formation.

Pl.42 : Region B – Alluvium deposit.

Pl.43 : Rim portion of Black and Red ware from Parikal.

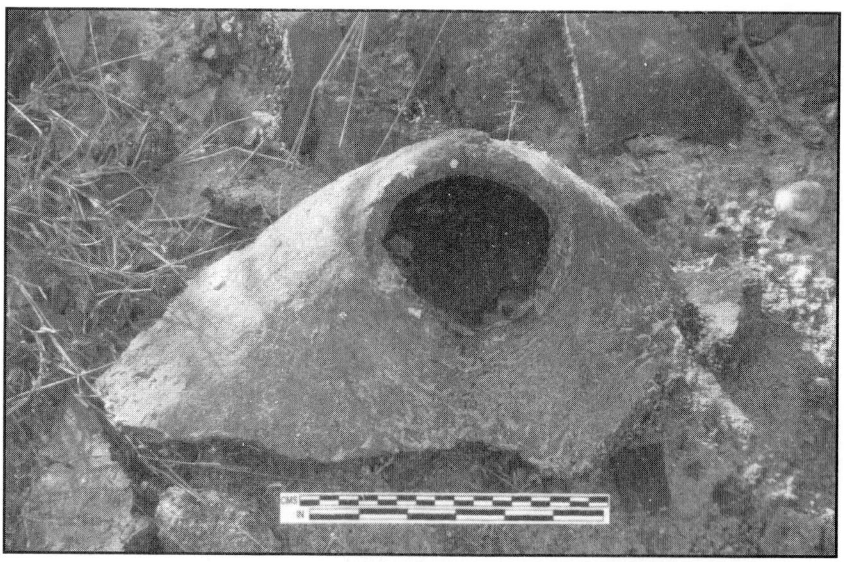

Pl.44 : Parikal – Coarse Red ware.

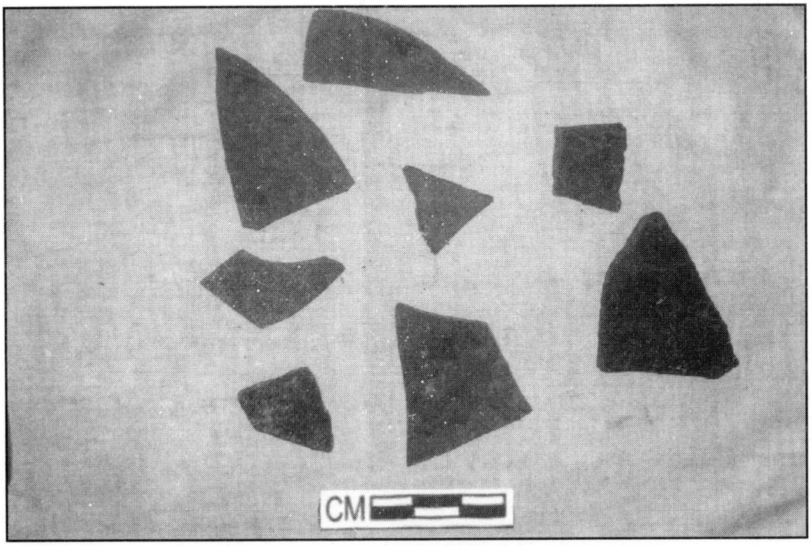

Pl.45 : Tirasu – Rouletted sherds.

Pl.46 : Karaimedu – Rouletted sherds.

Pl.47 : Manikolai – Red polished ware.

Pl.48 : Arikamedu – Fragment of Roman amphora jar.

Pl.49 : Arikamedu – Fragments of amphora jars.

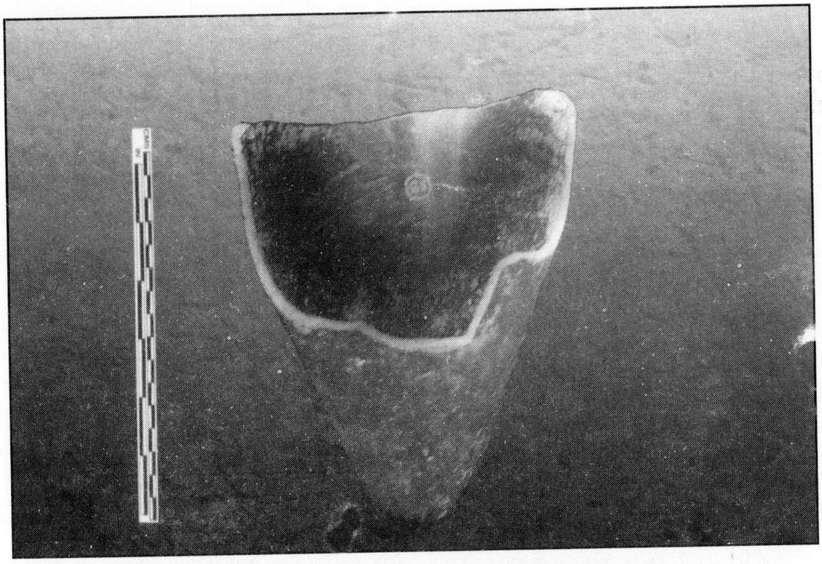

50 : Conical jar piece from Vasuvasamudram.

Pl.51 : Conical jar piece from Thirusopuram.

Pl.52 : Graffiti on Black and Red ware from Parikal.

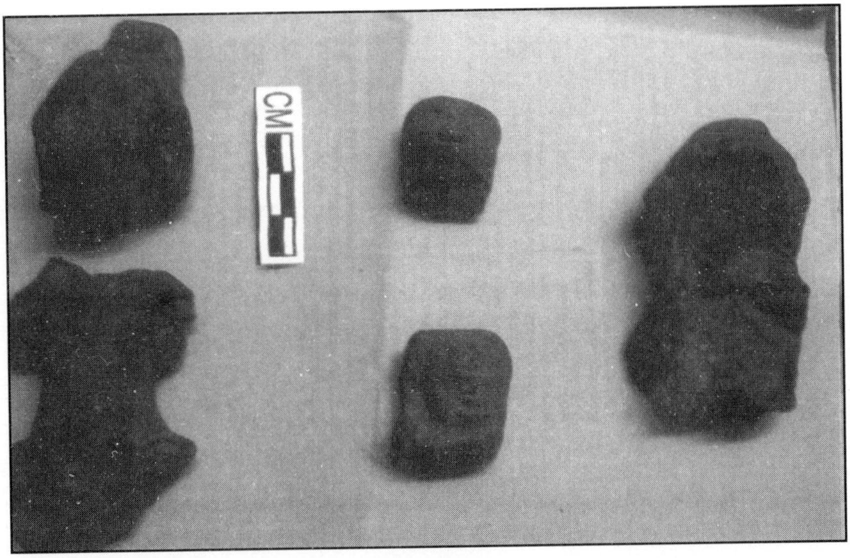

Pl.53 : Terracotta figurines – Kattusellur.

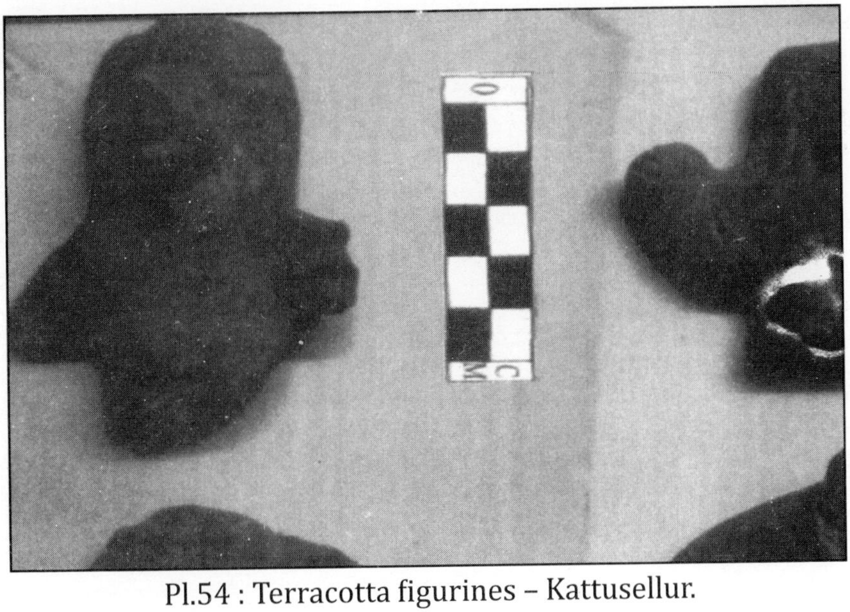

Pl.54 : Terracotta figurines – Kattusellur.

Pl.55 : Terracotta figurines – Kattusellur.

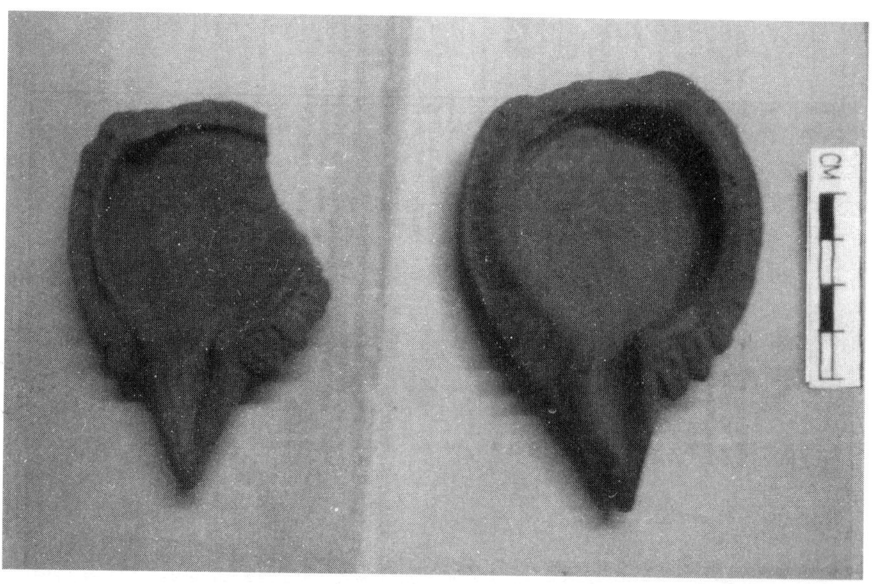

Pl.56 : Terracotta lamps - Arasur.

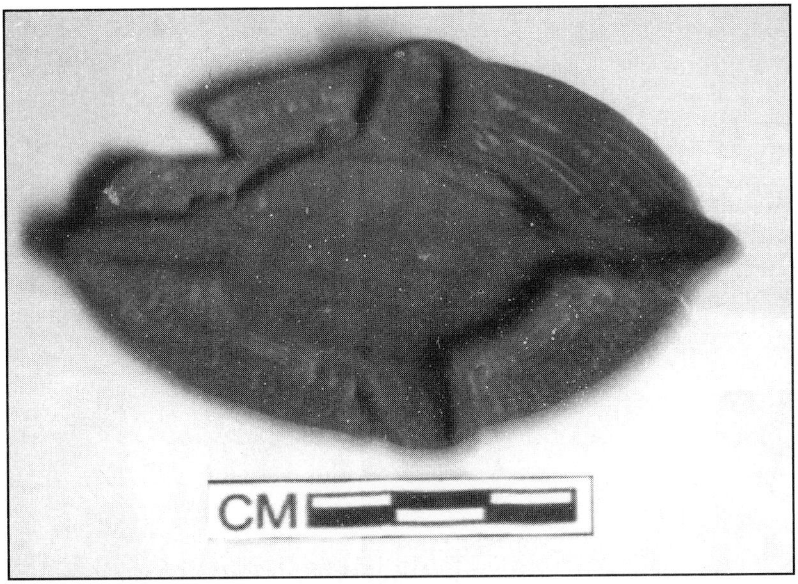

Pl.57 : Terracotta lamp – Sendiyampakkam.

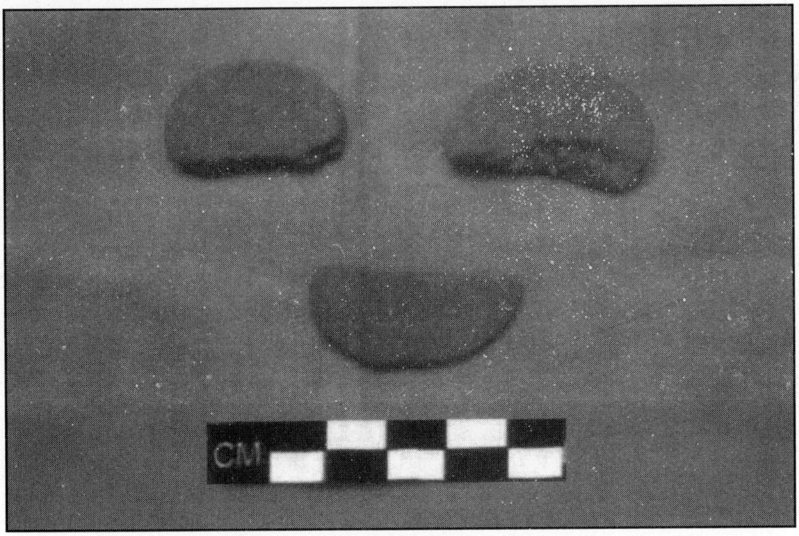

Pl.58: Tirsau – Hopscotchs.

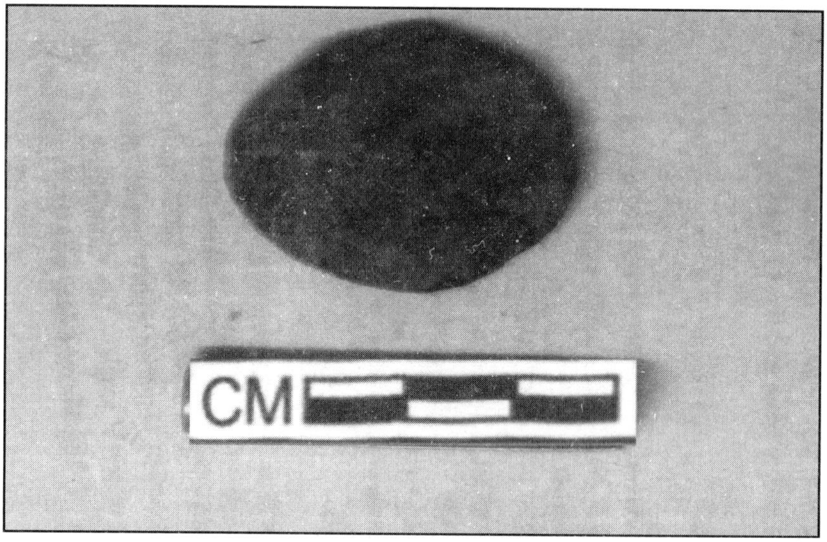

Pl.59 : Puvaram Kuppam – Hopscotch.

Pl.60 : Lid knobs and other Terracotta objects.

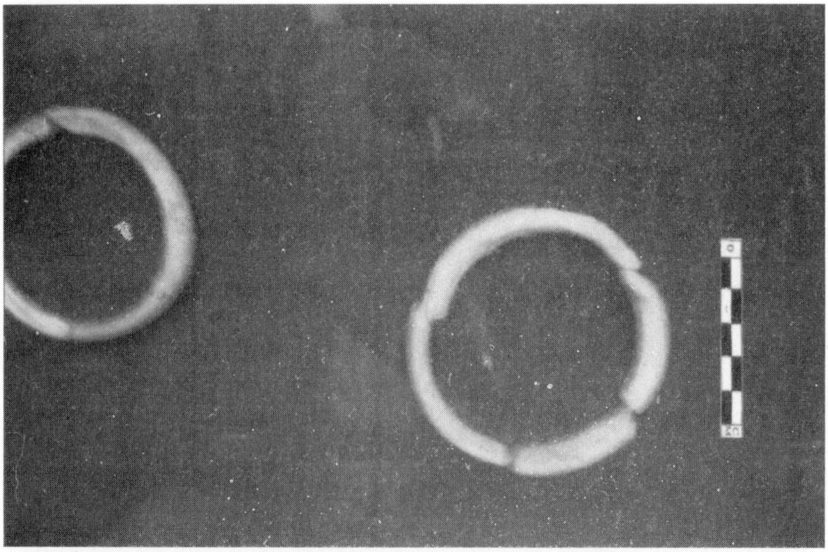

Pl.61 : Arikamedu – Shell bangles.

Pl.62 : Ulakkur – Core of shell (columella).

Suttukeni

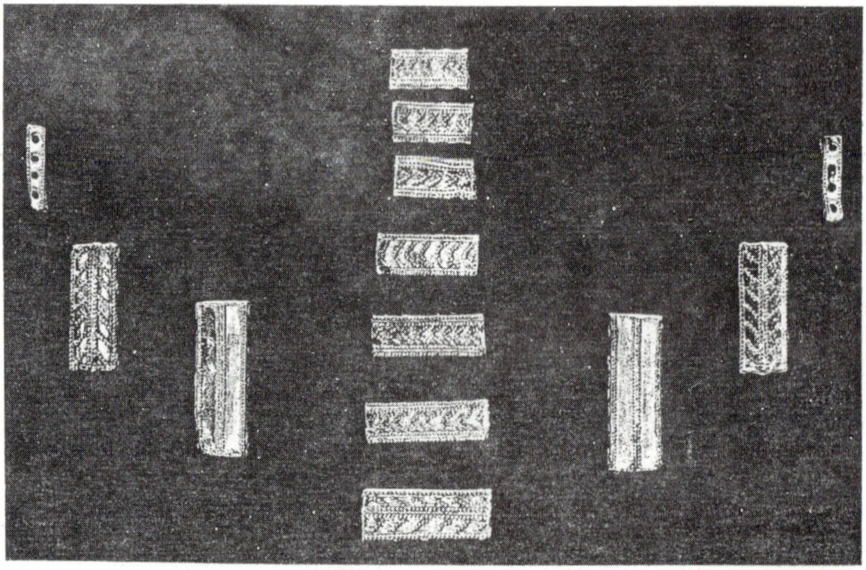

←(a)

THE 1989-92 EXCAVATIONS AT ARIKAMEDU

(b)→

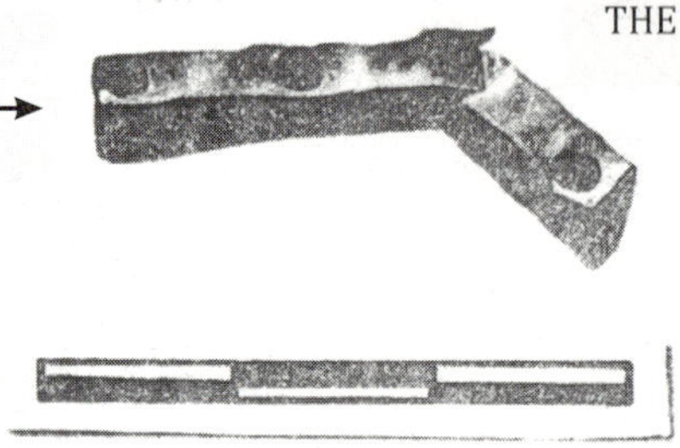

Gold necklace strand separator, broken and bent. Weight 1.7 grams.
50 B.C.-A.D. 25. Photo: V.Begley

Pl. 63 :
(a) Gold Necklace strand separator from Suttukeni.
(b) Similar Gold strand separator from Arikamedu.